Environmental Sustainability:
A Responsibility For All

Environmental Sustainability: A Responsibility For All

An Investigation of the U.S. Passenger Car Industry

Mary Gresens

Washington, DC

Copyright © 2012 by Mary Gresens
New Academia Publishing 2012

All rights reserved. No part of this book may be reproduced or transmitted in any form or by any means, electronic or mechanical, including photocopying, recording, or by any information storage and retrieval system.

Printed in the United States of America

Library of Congress Control Number: 2012942289
ISBN 978-0-9855698-5-3 paperback (alk. paper)

New Academia Publishing
PO Box 27420, Washington, DC 20038-7420
info@newacademia.com - www.newacademia.com

To Jen and Mark and new generations
A.M.D.G.

Contents

Acknowledgements		ix
Introduction		xi
I.	The Kantian Case for a *Sui Generis* Duty with Regard to the Environment	1
II.	Climate Change, Technology, and the U.S. Passenger Car Industry	9
III.	The U.S. Passenger Car System	27
IV.	Peril or Promise: Future Possibilities for the U.S. Passenger Car Industry	79
Reference List		133

Acknowledgements

I wish to thank all who have helped me along the way.

I am deeply grateful to my professors who urged me to question, learn, synthesize my ideas, and write.

John A. Resucher, my Doctor of Liberal Studies (DLS) Chair at Georgetown University, was the driving force behind me as we worked together on my doctoral thesis. He was relentless in his pursuit of intellectual originality and a great help in solidifying my thoughts and ideas into a cohesive work. Without his gentle, yet firm guidance, I would not have completed the thesis in the time we had agreed to. More importantly, he helped me learn to appreciate and understand Kant's words and works in a deep and meaningful fashion.

Terrence P. Reynolds was the conduit to the deeper questions concerning human values. His classes in Theology and Human Values and his assistance in formulating and writing the thesis as a member of my DLS Committee helped me define the issue of the value of human life in a distinct fashion. His classroom manner, characterized by respectful probing and questioning, has helped me focus on and refine my thoughts and personal interpretation of the meaning of life.

Wilfried Ver Eecke, a philosopher with a keen mind for business issues, was a great help in developing the concepts related to the intersection of human values and business-related matters. He was an invaluable member of my DLS Committee.

Francis J. Ambrosio introduced me to the concept of postmodernism. As a member of the DLS Executive Committee and one of my professors at Georgetown, he provided essential input for my understanding of the issues I had chosen to address with regard to our place in time and wth consideration of the possibility of the coexistence of incommensurate ideologies.

The late James N. Rosenau was my mentor during the Master of International Practice and Policy Program at The George Washington University. He helped me understand and apply what I had learned as an engineer and businesswoman in the context of an interconnected, global geopolitical system characterized by increasing complexity and the erosion of central authority.

Anna Lawton and Carole Sargent have provided much support and guidance as I enter into the world of publishing.

I also wish to thank three dear friends for their support, open ears, and patience during my time in the doctoral program: Sigrid, Joyce, and Anne.

I thank Richard, a great designer and a dear friend for his creation of the cover artwork,

Finally, I thank Jen, Mark, Jean, and Pi for their support and love throughout this project and other endeavors.

Introduction

As a child, I lived in Michigan, surrounded by the natural beauty of the Great Lakes. I spent my summers on Long Island, Maine located in Casco Bay. I learned to love nature. Both of my childhood homes were hard hit by the effects of catastrophies due to man-made causes. In June of 1969, the Cuyahoga River, flowing through Cleveland, Ohio and then to Lake Erie, caught on fire because it was so polluted. Not long thereafter, on July 22, 1972, the oil tanker Tomano stuck ground in Casco Bay, Maine spewing thousands of barrels of oil into the waters of the bay which landed on the shores of my beloved island.

I grew up in the Motor City and learned to love cars. I eventually entered the automotive industry where I worked for some thirty years as an engineer and business executive. During the course of my automotive career, I became increasingly aware of the effects of our desire for individual mobility on the environment. I was also able to learn about the development and deployment of technologies which could reduce the impact of automotive emissions. I experienced first-hand decisions which many companies made in favor of cost reduction to the detriment of the introduction of an environmentally friendly technology.

My most recent position was President of the Automotive Division and subsequently, Chief Financial Officer of one of the largest global automotive suppliers, and a leader in developing and producing environment-friendly technology, the Schaeffler Group. After retiring in 2006, I assumed ownership and became Chief Executive Officer of Barefoot Motors. The company designed and produced electric All Terrain Vehicles for agriculture and various land management sectors. In 2010, I made the decision to cease operations. The ATV market was heading into a period characterized by intense competition and price discounting. Again I witnessed the tradeoff of price versus eco-friendly vehicle technology. This time, it was my company which suffered along with the environment.

My latest educational endeavors complemented and deepened the lessons of my professional experience. In the Master of International Practice and Policy Program at The George Washington University, from which I graduated in 2008, I concentrated on international policy issues related to resource scarcity. The Doctor of Liberal Studies Program at Georgetown University, with its focus on human values, provided a deeper understanding of our human nature, the historical development of modern western thought, and the value of life.

As I developed the theme of my dissertation, which is the basis for this book, it became clear that the parties contributing to the emissions problem were a set of interacting players—a system. It also became increasingly evident that the portrayal of this system and the related environmental and resource issues as described in this work is a unique interdisciplinary synthesis of philosophy, scientific data related to climate change, automotive technology, domestic policy, and socio-historical information. My professors and publishers were also aware of the importance of this original intellectual contribution and have been insistent that I publish the work. Thanks to their support and persistence, I am now completing this version of my original dissertation which was submitted in May 2011.

Since that time, new data and information which confirm and support my theses contained in this work have become available. This is heartening as it underscores the message I deliver, yet at the same time it is alarming while it illustrates another of my tenets. Namely, that while we are cognizant that carbon dioxide emissions from passenger vehicles are having a lasting and negative impact on our climate and human health, we continue to do little to mitigate the harm we have caused and continue to cause.

The moral aspect of environmental sustainability has yet to be adequately addressed with regard to the passenger car sector. Almost all aspects of this industry involve decisions in which trade-offs are made between needs and wants. I maintain that we all, as human beings, have a binding and inter-generational moral duty to ensure the availability of those natural resources necessary for human existence.

This, however, is not as clear cut as it seems. Since the rise of modernity in Western society, and most recently in the post- modern era, we have been confronted with a discussion which questions the quintessence of central authority. This is compounded by modern technologies which allow for the formation of groups which often threaten or supersede any central authority. This higher order of complexity has significant implications for the application of a universal moral law with respect to future generations.

I argue this in four steps. Via an analysis of Kant's case for the Categorical Imperative as an objective basis for universal and binding moral decision-making, I show that if Kant's argument holds for an individual, it must necessarily be binding for all human beings, regardless of their place in time, a *sui generis* duty.

Second, I rely on selected primary sources and data to show that we are experiencing an environmental crisis, focusing on the aspect of climate change due to green house gas (GHG) emissions in the form of carbon dioxide (CO_2) emissions from passenger cars. I show that this threat is self-induced and controllable through concerted human activity to abate climate change concentrating on two aspects related to the U.S. passenger car industry - the contribution to CO_2 emissions and emissions flattening.

Third, I argue that this industrial sector (oil industry, automobile manufacturers, government, and consumers) is a system in which central authority is increasingly ineffective by presenting a historical analysis of the interrelationships within the sector, between the participant groups. I will show that these relationships are dependent on the motivational and situational forces in which each group finds itself and that these have changed over time. I will also show that if there is one common motivation shared by these groups, it is economic in nature and is measured by the costs and benefits which each of the groups believe to accrue to them, based on their evaluation of their situation.

Finally, I present a brief discussion of the post modern condition, which is characterized by a lack of central authority. I maintain that there is both promise and peril in this present situation, as higher-level behavior is almost impossible to predict in advance. I will suggest measures for technical solutions as well as short- and mid-term policies which may lead to longer term results and possibilities for us to protect the environment for future generations.

I do not have a concrete answer, but hope, through this discussion to raise awareness of the complex and interrelated issues involved and to generate a new understanding of the problem in an attempt to contribute to the effort to save our planet for future generations.

In addition to the use of primary and secondary sources, I will incorporate information which was introduced in various courses during my studies. In the parenthetical references, I will cite the information presented in this form by noting the professor's name and year in which I attended the lecture. The Reference List will contain this information as well as the course number and title and the term in which the course was held. I will also use information from certain corporations, automobile manufacturers and automotive suppliers, which is publically available. The use of this information is not intended to promote the interest of nor negatively position any specific company, but rather, to serve as examples, facts, products, technologies, and policies which impact the environment.

I am also writing a trade version of this scholarly book, which will be available for publication later this year. I would like to reach yet a wider audience with this second book in the hope to increase collective awareness with the result that efforts to preserve the environment for our children and following generations garner broader participation and increased support.

I.

The Kantian Case for a *Sui Generis* Duty with Regard to the Environment

The purpose of this chapter is to provide a philosophical argument for the claim that there exists a collective moral obligation binding each generation to care for the next generation's access to the resources it needs to flourish. I refer specifically to needs rather than wants. I define needs as those physical, psychological, and social elements in human life which have to be fulfilled to obtain and maintain an adequate state of health and well-being.

Wants, conversely, may be desires which exceed these needs and often result in over-consumption of any factor of well being. While there are many needs which are requisite for human life to flourish, such as sufficient income to sustain life, education, and a socio-political system which allows for freedom and individual development, I believe we have reached a point in time where the basic needs of human existence are being threatened - those resources which future generations will require to live - air, water, and food. This threat is self-induced and controllable through concerted human activity to abate climate change (Dessler and Parson 2007, 158).

Provided we can do something, two questions follow: what can be done and why should we act. This chapter will focus on the second aspect - why - What should or ought we do? The word "ought" is perhaps one of the most misused words in the contemporary English language. The Merriam-Webster Dictionary defines ought as a verb "used to express obligation, advisability, natural expectation, or logical consequence" and also as a noun which refers to "moral obligation or duty" (*Merriam Webster Dictionary, Online ed.,* s.v. "ought"). Today, the correct grammatical use of the word has become diffuse and is focused almost exclusively on the verbal definition, with the result that term is often used to denote something as being vaguely prescriptive, even if the matter discussed has no prescriptive quality. Greene notes that there is even disagreement in the field of moral philosophy as evidenced by the fact that some moral ethicists question the distinction between the neuroscientific "is" and the moral philosophical "ought" (Greene 2003, 847).

I will rely on Immanuel Kant's development of the ought, the Categorical Imperative, and use it as at least one of the principles which can be employed to provide an objective basis for moral decisions regarding binding and collective inter-generational moral obligation. I will use the terms Categorical Imperative and universal and absolute law interchangeably in the ensuing discussion. My use of this principle will be based on selected works of Kant, including, *Critique of Pure Reason, Grounding for the Metaphysics of Morals, Critique of Practical Reason, The Metaphysics of Morals, Religion and Rational Theology,* and *Lectures on Ethics*. I will present my argument in two steps. First, I will provide an analysis of Kant's case for the Categorical Imperative as the objective basis for moral decision making. In the second step, I will show that if Kant's argument holds for an individual by virtue of his humanness, it must necessarily be binding for all human beings, as persons, regardless of their place in time.

Central to the understanding of the Categorical Imperative is the notion of title. We have rights by virtue of what we are - persons - autonomous agents. We have title because a person belongs to himself by virtue of the autonomy of his self consciousness (Reuscher 2010). The use of the masculine gender includes all persons. According to Kant, reason, as the basis of autonomy, is why human beings are the object of respect. Respect is the acknowledgement of the absolute value of the human being and that absolute value is freedom (Kant 1993b, 10). Our human insight shows us what is reasonable - what one or everyone ought to do. This insight of reason is the essence of our human freedom. We are the only free agents on this earth because we can reason and can choose to act according to reason. Animals act according to instinct (Kant 1993b, 13). Precisely this human ability to decide to act and the basis of the decision of how to act highlights our freedom to choose to do good in and of itself (Kant 1993b, 7). The goodness is an absolute value of the will and not dependent on the quality of the results (Kant 1993b, 8).

Kant maintains that duty includes good will, a sense of obligation (Kant 1993b, 9). Action arising from duty has a moral worth in the maxim according to which the action is determined by the individual (Kant 1993b, 12). Kant's discussion of the foundations for decision-making provides the basis for the Categorical Imperative, the ought. Maxims are the class of foundations for decisions which are outside of the realm of logic, but they are decisions from which nothing follows (Kant, 1993b, 12). Kant distinguishes between maxims and those decisions of moral worth, noting two important distinguishing factors. First, the moral decision involves an *a priori* principle, which is formal and second, that there is no *a posteriori* incentive, i.e. material, which is determined by volition rather than duty (Kant 1993b, 13). He continues and builds the bridge to the ought:

> Hence, there is nothing left which can determine the will except objectively the law and subjectively pure reason for this practical law, i.e., the will can be subjectively determined by the maxim that I should follow such a law even if all my inclinations are thwarted....Therefore the pre-eminent good which is called moral can consist in nothing but the representation of the law itself and such a representation can admittedly be found only in a rational being insofar as the representation, and not some expected effect, is the determining ground of the will. (Kant 1993b, 13-14)

Kant proceeds to define the Categorical Imperative based upon the above development of how a reasonable human agent makes decisions based upon his perceptions. In making a decision where the will "has been deprived of every impulse that may arise" (Kant 1993b, 14), i.e. volition,"there is nothing left to serve the will as principle except the universal conformity of its actions to law as such, i.e., I should never act except in such a way that I can also will that my maxim should become a universal law" (Kant 1993b, 14). Kant then continues to refine this definition of the ought and clearly binds the legislative universality of action to the autonomy of the will: "Hence, morality is the relation of actions to the autonomy of the will, i.e., the possible legislation of the universal law by means of the maxims of the will. That action which is compatible with the autonomy of the will is permitted; that which is not compatible is forbidden" (Kant 1993b, 44).

In *Critique of Practical Reason,* Kant describes this form of legislation as the making of law in such a way that it is prescriptive, i.e. it gives moral content to the decision (Kant 1993a, 26). He maintains that the decision- making process should always be based on the maxim which provides for moral law - the Categorical Imperative. This decision can only be based on insight, the root of human agency grounded in freedom and respect, and not feelings or want (Kant 1993a, 26). It is here, in *Critique of Practical Reason,* that Kant goes beyond the self consciousness in the scientific sense to his argument of reason as a source of necessity because it is prescriptive (Kant 1993a, 29) - the ought - and that the source of law is the ability of the mind to reason (Kant 1993a, 31). Basic to this argument is the understanding of "I want" as opposed to "I ought". Kant maintains that wanting is a fundamental human temptation. When the want has replaced the ought, it has substituted motivation for freedom and the person is deceived by the self that the I is want in the form of freedom (Kant 1993a, 79). For Kant, the "I want" is the antithesis of freedom (Reuscher 2010) and the denial of our humanness (Reynolds 2009).

In *The Metaphysics of Morals,* Kant delves further into this theme and describes the ends which are also duties, and thus brings unity to his argument. Keeping in mind that, for Kant, perfection is the realization of our absolute freedom, for him these ends, which are duties are, "one's own perfection and the happiness of others. Perfection and happiness cannot be interchanged, so that one's own perfection and the happiness of others would be made ends that would be in themselves duties of the same person " (Kant 1996, 150). According to Kant, this leads to "an all inclusive circle of world citizens who promote not "as the end what is best for the world but only to cultivate what leads indirectly to this end: to cultivate a disposition of reciprocity – agreeableness, tolerance, mutual love and respect (affability and propriety, *humanitas aesthetica et decorum)* – and so to associate the graces with virtue. To bring this about is, itself, a duty of virtue" (Kant 1996, 218). This is the bridge to Kant's argument for a *sui generis* binding moral obligation.

Kant asserts, however, that the maintenance of morality is a struggle akin to war, "in which the good principle, which resides in each human being, is incessantly attacked by the evil found within him and in every other as well" (Kant 2005, 132). In order to fulfill our duty, according to Kant, we must win this war. As noted above, Kant maintains that one's own perfection and the happiness of others are one's personal duty (Kant 1996, 150) and that we, as human beings, have a duty of virtue to bring this about (Kant 1996, 218).

In *Religion and Rational Theology*, Kant maintains that this is a *sui generis* duty, "not of human beings toward human beings, but of the human race toward itself" (Kant 2005, 132). The greatest moral perfection, according to Kant in *Letters on Ethics*, is the ultimate destiny of the human race, provided that it is achieved through human freedom, where by alone man is capable of the greatest happiness." He maintains that we must each make a contribution to the ultimate destiny of mankind (Kant 1993c, 252). As rational beings we are "destined to a common end" which is the promotion of the highest moral good which cannot be obtained through the pursuit of individual moral perfection but only through a community of persons trying to achieve the highest moral good, "a universal republic based on laws of virtue" (Kant, 1993c, 252). By definition, this community must be self-legislative and the legislation is based on the principle of "limiting the freedom of each to the conditions under which it can coexist with the freedom of everyone else, in conformity with universal law" (Kant 1993c, 252).

While we may be well aware of this, it is not an easy task to deal with ethical issues. There exist multitudes of information and data. By virtue of pure informational volume, the empirical food for thought and possible solutions - what is, was, or will be - outweigh the moral claims what "ought" to be done. In the U.S., our society and our politics are highly influenced by incrementalism and logical positivism, as evidenced by our fascination with the market economy and science. Only empirical claims are empirically testable and verifiable and are, therefore, considered to be cognitively meaningful. In addition, open recognition of morality often has a poor reputation in our society. Those who moralize are often viewed as having to make harsh and often unreasonable judgments. The fact that we tend to seek win-win situations compounds the problem.

Sagoff, identifying with Kant, maintains that there is an inherent problem in using economic models to define and determine actions which are intrinsic to our present economic model of success. This arises from using cost-benefit analyses to determine values. The values thus determined can only be values which are linked to market price values or contemporary interpretation of what is truly valuable. According to Sagoff, "It is the characteristic of cost-benefit analysis that it treats all value judgments other than those made on its behalf as nothing but statements of preference, attitude, or emotion, insofar as they are value judgments. The cost-benefit analyst regards as true the judgment that we should maximize efficiency or wealth" (Sagoff 1998, 331). As he notes, we tend to want to reduce all decisions to a type of data-based decision or a cost-benefit analysis (Sagoff 1998, 330).

Sagoff posits that when we use the market model as the basis of all decisions, we are "ignoring competing visions of what a society should be like" (Sagoff 2003, 334) and manage society as a market in which individuals trade freely and in which there is no central authority - neither a particular individual person, belief, or faith. He maintains that we cannot replace moral law with economic analysis because "the antinomianism of cost-benefit analysis is not enough" (Sagoff 1998, 334).

If, as discussed in this section on Kant's moral philosophy, human life is absolutely valuable, then there can be no bargaining about its absolute worth. Second, aside from our lack of comfort in dealing with issues which do not lead to the desired market-based end, morally significant considerations arise when options are under consideration that may possibly harm those subject to them. Harm can be considered to be pain, lack of means or opportunity to fulfill an individual's needs, or even possible health problems or in the extreme, death. Situations which are morally difficult tend to be those in which all alternatives, including doing nothing, involve causing or allowing harm to a human being, including those of the present and future generations (VanDeVeer and Pierce 2003, 12).

According to Kant, the individual is a judge of values, not a "mere haver of wants" (Sagoff 1998, 332) and the individual judges not merely for himself, but as a member of a community. In doing so, he recognizes that values are subjective states of mind but that they are also objective in nature and are either therefore correct or mistaken - they are cognitive. Therefore, a person who makes a value judgment claims to know what is right, not just what is preferred. A value judgment is like an empirical or theoretical judgment in that it claims to be true. The neutrality of the economic approach is legitimate if private preferences and wants are the only values under consideration. However, cost-benefit analyses treat people only "as locations at which wants may be found" and fail to treat them as value-havers and therefore are not a basis for legitimacy as such analyses and their results do not consider and are indifferent to true human values (Sagoff 1998, 333).

Kant compelling shows that, if we are to maintain our absolute value as human beings, we cannot be parts of an equation which has as its goal to weigh what has more economic worth. For, if we, as the only free agents on this planet, deny or are denied our absolute worth, there is no basis for morality.

I have shown, through an investigation of Kant's moral philosophy, that we all have a binding moral duty to promote our own perfection and the happiness of others. If this holds for the individual by virtue of his human agency, then it must hold collectively for all human beings, present and future. Therefore, there exists a binding, intergenerational moral law and duty. This obligation is not contingent on the time participation of people in history, but a moral law which requires that we must always act in the interest of all mankind, those human beings present today and those to come. This necessarily includes protecting the environment to ensure that all have adequate resources which are a requisite for human life.

II.

Climate Change, Technology, and the U.S. Passenger Car Industry

The focus of this section of Chapter II will be on GHG emissions in the form of atmospheric carbon dioxide (CO_2) as this is the main pollutant emitted by passenger cars and also because it is measureable and directly related to fuel consumption. This will provide a basis for the following discussion of technological possibilities to reduce CO_2 emissions. (Note: The term passenger cars, when used referring to the U.S. industry, includes all vehicles typically classified as passenger cars in this country, including minivans, sport utility vehicles (SUVs) and pickup trucks).

According to the U.S. Environmental Protection Agency (EPA), "In addition to carbon dioxide, automobiles produce methane (CH_4) and nitrous oxide (N_2O) from the tailpipe, as well as HFC [hydroflurocarbon] emissions from leaking air conditioners. The emissions of CH_4 and N_2O are related to vehicle miles traveled rather than fuel consumption, and the emissions of CH_4, N_2O, and HFCs are not as easily estimated from a vehicle as for CO_2. On average, CH_4, N_2O, and HFC emissions represent roughly 5-6 percent of the GHG emissions from passenger vehicles, while CO_2 emissions account for 94-95 percent, accounting for the global warming potential of each greenhouse gasoline" (EPA 2005, 4).

CO_2 Emissions From Past to Present

A historical review of the tracking of global atmospheric CO_2 from all sources of emissions shows that it varied between 260 and 285 parts per million (ppm) since the dawn of the agricultural age until the beginning of the Industrial Revolution in the United Kingdom in the 1800s (Heinzerling 2010). Since that time, as can be seen in the following illustration, over the course of the last two-and-a half-centuries, the level has risen rapidly to over 389.69 ppm on December 31, 2010 (CO2 Now 2011).

As recently reported by the Earth Policy Institute, "The last time carbon dioxide levels were this high was roughly 15 million years ago, when the sea level was 25-40 meters (80-130 feet) higher and global temperatures were 3-6 degrees Celsius (5-11 degrees Fahrenheit) warmer" than today (Heinzerling 2010).

Illustration 1. Historical Global CO_2 Emissions Levels

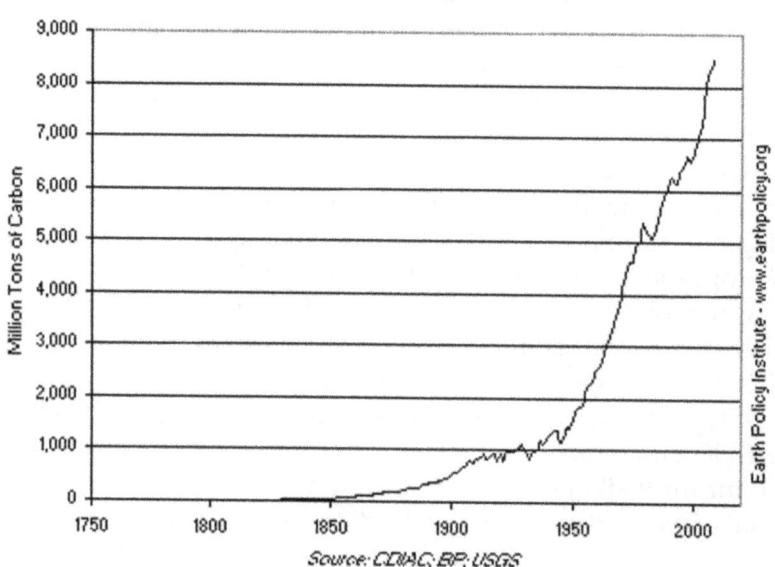

(Note: Each part per million of CO_2 corresponds to a total of 2.1 billion tons of atmospheric carbon)
Source: Heinzerling, 2010.

The National Oceanic and Atmospheric Administration (NOAA), a federal agency focused on the condition of the oceans and the atmosphere, has tracked global CO_2 atmospheric concentrations at the Mauna Loa Observatory since 1958. As can be seen in Illustration 2, the data show that the global mean annual level of atmospheric CO_2, as measured in ppm, has risen from 315.9 ppm in 1960 to a level of 389.78 ppm as of December 2010 (NOAA 2011). The level of 350 ppm, which is deemed to be the threshold level for risk to human health (Gang He 2008), was passed in January 1988. This rise in atmospheric CO_2 has been accompanied by a rise in atmospheric temperature. As reported by Eiplerin in *The Washington Post*, the NASA Goddard Institute for Space Studies reported that the first six months of 2010 were the warmest on record, "both in terms of atmospheric data and in combined atmospheric/ocean readings". Temperatures were between 1.8 and 3.6 degrees Fahrenheit warmer than in previous years. At the same time, the Arctic sea ice extent reached the lowest level ever for June (Eilperin 2010, E3).

Illustration 2. Global Atmospheric CO_2 Levels 1960-2010 Annual Mean Concentration (ppm)

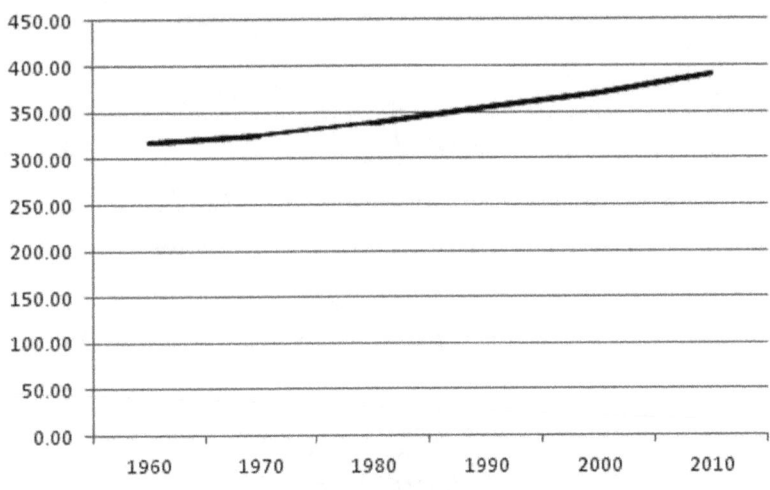

Source: Atmospheric CO2 Mauna Loa Observatory NOAA

As depicted below in Illustration 3, the US held the position of leading global CO_2 emitter until 2009 when it was surpassed by China. According to the Earth Policy Institute, "In 2009, carbon dioxide (CO2) emissions in China - the world's leading emitter - grew by nearly 9 percent. At the same time, emissions in most industrial countries dropped, bringing global CO2 emissions from fossil fuel use down from a high of 8.5 billion tons of carbon in 2008 to 8.4 billion tons in 2009. Yet this drop follows a decade of rapid growth: over the 10 previous years, global CO2 emissions rose by an average of 2.5 percent a year - nearly four times as fast as in the 1990s" (Heinzerling 2010).

Although the U.S. is no longer the leading source of total CO_2 emissions, our country is still the leader in these emissions on a per capita basis, as reported by the World Bank last year. The U.S. emits

Illustration 3. Atmospheric CO_2 Levels - U.S. and China in MMTC

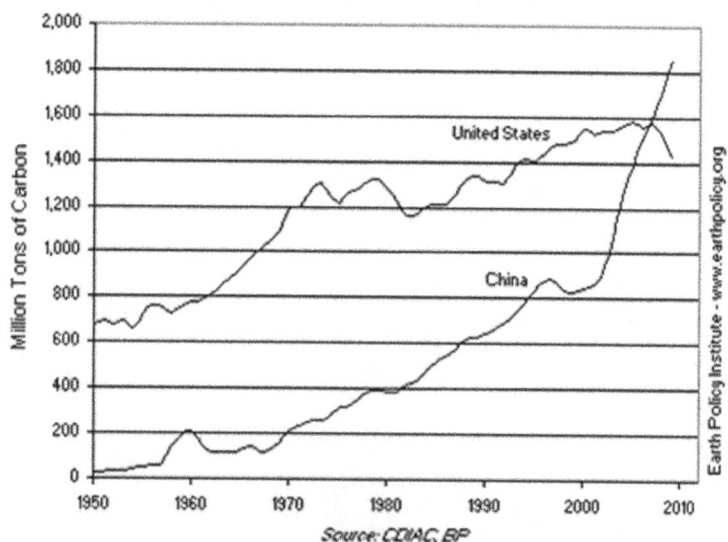

Source: Heinzerling, 2010

Illustration 4. CO_2 Emissions - U.S. and World Average in Metric Tons per Capita

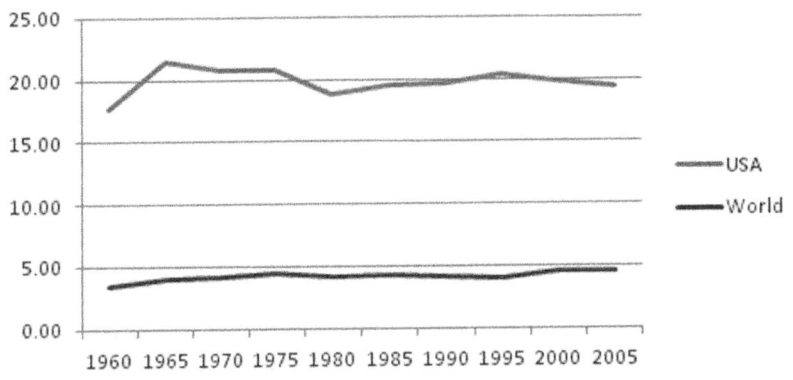

Source: World Bank 2010

19.94 metric tons per capita on average in comparison to the global average of 4.63, as shown in Illustration 4 (World Bank 2010).

Even though the U.S. per capita CO_2 emissions have increased at a slower rate than the global average since 1960, 2.1 percent versus 4.3 percent, respectively, the U.S. average increase of 0.32 metric tons per capita in that same period is more than twice the global average increase of 0.15 metric tons per capita (Table 1, p. 14).

In the EPA's 2010 issue of *U.S. Inventory of Greenhouse Gas Emissions and Sinks*, it was reported that total U.S. GHG emissions in 2008 were 6,9568.8 teragrams of CO_2 equivalents (Tg CO_2 Eq) and that net emissions were 6,016.4 Tg CO_2 Eq, reflecting the positive contribution of sink effects due to land usage and forestry. However, U.S. total emissions increased almost 14 percent from 1990 through 2008, although a decrease from 2007-2008 was seen, mainly due to a decrease in electricity demand and energy demand due to higher energy prices (EPA 2010a, 2-1).

The EPA further reported that the greatest source of U.S. GHG CO_2 emissions is from fossil fuel combustion and that this source "has accounted for approximately seventy nine percent of global warming potential (GWP) weighted emissions since 1990 growing from seven percent of GWP in 1990 to 80 percent in 2008" and that

Table 1. CO_2 Emissions - U.S. and World in Metric Tons per Capita

Year	USA	World	US Increase	USA Increase as %	World Increase	World Increase as %
1960	16.16	3.11				
1965	17.71	3.47	1.55	9.6%	0.36	11.6%
1970	21.50	4.05	3.79	21.4%	0.58	16.7%
1975	20.71	4.15	-0.79	-3.7%	0.10	2.5%
1980	20.76	4.38	0.05	0.2%	0.23	5.5%
1985	18.83	4.16	-1.93	-9.3%	-0.22	-5.0%
1990	19.47	4.27	0.64	3.4%	0.11	2.6%
1995	19.59	4.11	0.12	0.6%	-0.16	-3.7%
2000	20.33	4.06	0.74	3.8%	-0.05	-1.2%
2005	19.73	4.52	-0.60	-3.0%	0.46	11.3%
2007	19.34	4.63	-0.39	-2.0%	0.11	2.4%
Average	19.47	4.08	0.32	2.1%	0.15	4.3%

Source: World Bank 2010

"these emissions were responsible for most of the increase in national emissions during this period. Historically, changes in emissions from fossil fuel combustion have been the dominant factor affecting U.S. emission trends" (EPA 2010a). The EPA also notes that the annual changes in CO_2 emission vary, in the short term, according to growth in the population and the economy, as well as increases in energy prices and seasonal temperatures. Longer term influences include scale consumption patterns related to population, number of vehicles, and size of houses as well as the efficiency of the energy used and the carbon intensity of the fuel or energy used (EPA 2010a).

In that same report, dated July 2010, the EPA sector analysis of GHG, which includes the electricity-related emissions distributed to end-use sectors, indicates that the transportation sector accounted for 27 percent of GHG emissions and 30.8 percent of CO_2 emissions in the U.S. in 2008, whereby almost 100 percent of CO_2 emissions from the transportation sector were the result of direct emissions as shown in the following Table 2.

Table 2. U.S. GHG and CO$_2$ Emissions by Economic Sector with Electricity-Related Emissions Distributed in Tg CO$_2$ Eq – 2008

Sector	All GHGs	% US Total	CO$_2$	% US Total CO$_2$	CO$_2$ as % of all GHGs	% CO$_2$ direct emissions	% CO$_2$ electricity-related emissions
Industrial	2,018.4	29.0%	1718.7	29.4%	85.2%	61.1%	38.9%
Transportation	1,890.8	27.2%	1799.6	30.8%	95.2%	99.7%	0.3%
Commercial	1,250.6	18.0%	1050.7	18.0%	84.0%	20.9%	79.1%
Residential	1,215.6	17.5%	1190.4	20.4%	97.9%	28.8%	71.2%
Agriculture	531.6	7.6%	81.2	1.4%	15.3%	66.5%	33.5%
US Territories	49.9	0.7%	NA				
Total	6,956.9	100.0%	5,840.6	100.0%	84.0%		

Source: EPA 2010a

As indicated below in Table 3, the main contributors to all GHG and CO_2 emissions within the transportation sector were passenger cars (33 percent) and light trucks, which include sport utility vehicles (SUVs), pickup trucks, and minivans (29 percent) (EPA 2010a, 2-21). Considering this, passenger vehicles accounted for 62.6 percent of all transportation sector-related GHG emissions in the U.S. in 2008 and 61.7 percent of all transportation sector-related CO_2 emissions in the U.S. for the same period.

JATO Dynamics, a leading automotive research organization, compared the emissions statistics of the U.S. passenger car market for the first quarter of 2010 to two other car-intensive regions - Europe and Japan. The study showed that average CO_2 emissions from passenger vehicles in the U.S. were 268.5 grams per kilometer (g/km).When corrected to be comparable to the other markets, vehicles which are considered to be passenger cars in the U.S. and not classified as such in the other two markets, such as pickup trucks, full sized vans and small commercial vehicles were excluded and

Table 3. U.S. GHG and CO_2 Emission by Mode of Transportation in $TgCO_2Eq$ – 2008

	All GHGs	% Sector Total	CO_2	% Sector Total CO_2	CO_2 as % of all GHGs
Passenger Cars	632.1	33.4%	597.5	33.2%	94.5%
Light-Duty Trucks	552.4	29.2%	513.7	28.5%	93.0%
Medium/Heavy Duty Trucks	401.2	21.2%	388.6	21.6%	96.9%
Buses	12.1	0.6%	11.7	0.7%	96.7%
Motorcycles	2.2	0.1%	2.1	0.1%	95.5%
Aircraft	157.1	8.3%	155.5	8.6%	99.0%
Ships/Boats	38.7	2.0%	38.1	2.1%	98.4%
Rail	50.6	2.7%	47.9	2.7%	94.7%
Pipelines	34.9	1.8%	34.9	1.9%	100.0%
Lubricants	9.5	0.5%	9.5	0.5%	100.0%
Total	1,890.8	100.0%	1,799.5	100.0%	95.2%

Source: EPA 2010a

only passenger cars were included. The corrected U.S. CO_2 emissions for passenger cars were 255.6 g/km. European and Japanese passenger cars averaged 140.3 g/km and 130.8 g/km, respectively (JATO Dynamics, 2011).

When the fuel economy rating of the vehicles in the respective markets is taken into consideration, i.e. miles per gallon (mpg), the reason for this discrepancy is evident. In the U.S., 33.9 percent of all passenger vehicles sold fall within the 15-20 miles per gallon (mpg) range. In Japan only 0.63 percent of passenger cars sold offers such relatively low fuel economy. In Europe, the figure is even lower, 0.28 percent. One of the main reasons for this difference in Europe is the popularity of diesel-powered cars which have a market share of 48.9 percent in that region. The U.S. market, conversely, is "dominated by gasoline which has 81.9 percent market share with only 1.7 percent being diesel" (JATO Dynamics 2011). While the market share of diesel engines in Japan is only 0.11 percent, "the highly congested roads make very small and economical gasoline cars a popular choice" in Japan (JATO Dynamics 2011).

Future Scenarios for CO_2 Emissions

According to Dessler and Parson, a middle trajectory path with medium sensitivity and a temperature change of + 3°C would mean that emissions of GHG in developed countries, including the U.S , would need to be reduced to 60 percent below 2000 levels by 2050, provided developing countries begin to control emissions by 2030 (Dessler and Parson 2007, 158). Even stringent reduction of GHG to this level would expose us to significant risks and represents a 35-40 percent chance of passing the threshold of danger and still result in an overall increase in global temperatures requiring adaptive measures that represent sweeping changes to the way we presently live. It has been suggested that the climate change path we are on will lead to a reduction in our global supply of those resources necessary to maintain daily activity and that these shortages will lead to price increases at best and overt conflict at worst. Richard Wright addressed this issue as early as 1970 in his article, "Responsibility for the Ecological Crisis". He maintained that we are heading toward an environmental crisis of disastrous proportions due to two aspects which he considered destructive – overpopulation and technology. He claimed that we are unwilling to get these under control, although we have the means to do so (Wright 1970, 851-853). Almost thirty years later, Thomas Homer Dixon confirmed Wright's postulate and described how resource scarcity will lead to disruption and violence in his book, *Environment, Scarcity, and Violence* (Homer-Dixon 1999).

Three human factors have been shown to influence emission rates - population growth, economic growth, and technology. Dessler and Parson note that any effort to slow or reverse emission growth would have to achieve some combination in controlling one more of these trends. Within the technological realm there exist three main categories of solutions: land usage, increased efficiency of alternate energy sources used, and reduction of GHG based on updated existing technology (Dessler and Parson 2007, 158). This thesis focuses on the domestic passenger car sector and will therefore concentrate on the technology related factors in the automotive industry.

A major source of CO_2 is the burning of petroleum products to produce energy to power vehicles, to heat buildings, or to produce electric power by either direct or indirect turbine power. In the U.S., in contrast to other regions of the world where oil is more commonly used for space heating and power generation than for transportation, about 68 percent of all oil consumed is by the transportation sector. Gasoline accounts for about two-thirds of the total oil used for transportation in the U.S. (Dessler and Parson 2007, 158). As previously mentioned, the EPA notes that the primary driver of transportation-related emissions was "CO_2 from fossil fuel combustion, which increased by 20 percent from 1990 to 2008" (EPA 2010a, 2-21).

Socolow and Pacala have introduced the idea of a "stabilization wedge" as a tool to evaluate different CO_2 emission scenarios (Socolow and Pacala 2004, 968). They defined the emissions gap, or difference between the business-as-usual case and one that stabilizes the concentration of emissions and determined that it can be sliced into fifteen "stabilization wedges", each of which was defined as a specific activity that, over the next 50 years, could cumulatively reduce 25 billion tons of carbon emissions on a global level. Their wedge concept is depicted below in Illustration 5.

Climate Change   19

It was estimated that a combination of seven of these global-scale wedges would allow global emissions to be flattened over the next 50 years (Socolow and Pacala 2006, 50-57). This would mean that instead of rising to a global CO_2 emission level of over 850 ppm by 2050, emission levels could be contained at about 550 ppm. However, as previously noted, the level deemed safe for human health is 350 ppm (GangHe 2008). The flattening effort would bring

Illustration 5. The Stabilization Wedge

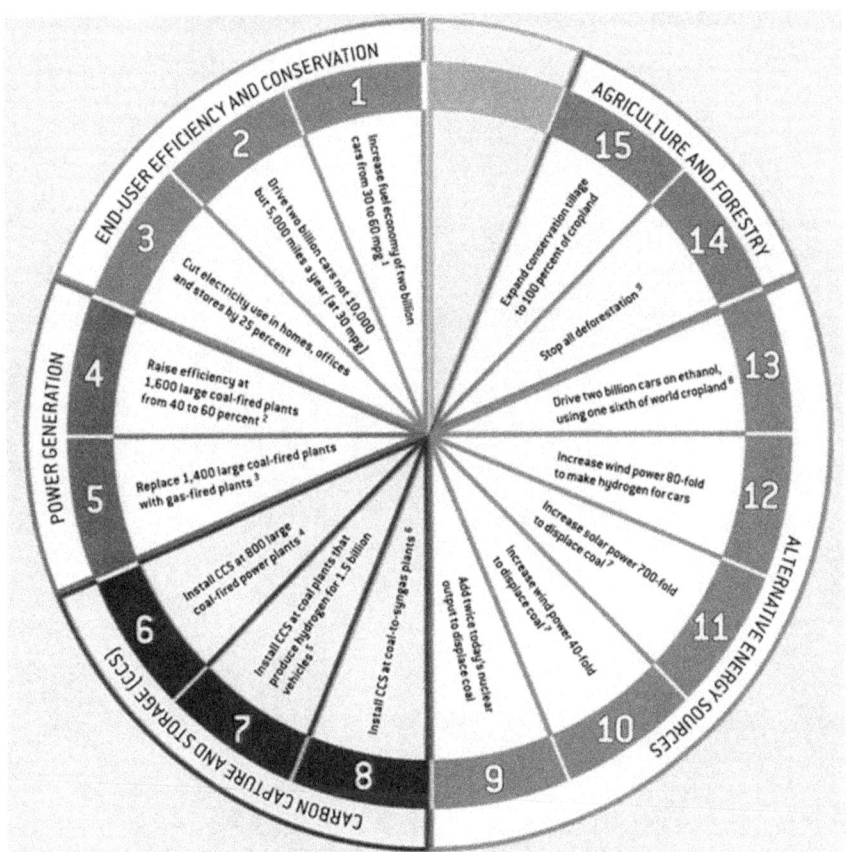

Source: Socolow and Pacala 2004

us to a level which is, at best, 57 percent above that level of risk, as seen in Illustration 6.

A team of scientists at the EPA applied Pacala's and Socolow's concept to an analysis of the U.S. transportation industry and identified nine wedges which they termed USTS (U.S. Transportation Sector) wedges, each capable of reducing 5,000 MMTC cumulative emissions by 2050 which together would flatten the emissions in the transportation sector. Half of these wedges would contribute sufficient reduction to flatten emissions from passenger vehicles

Illustration 6. The Wedge Solution

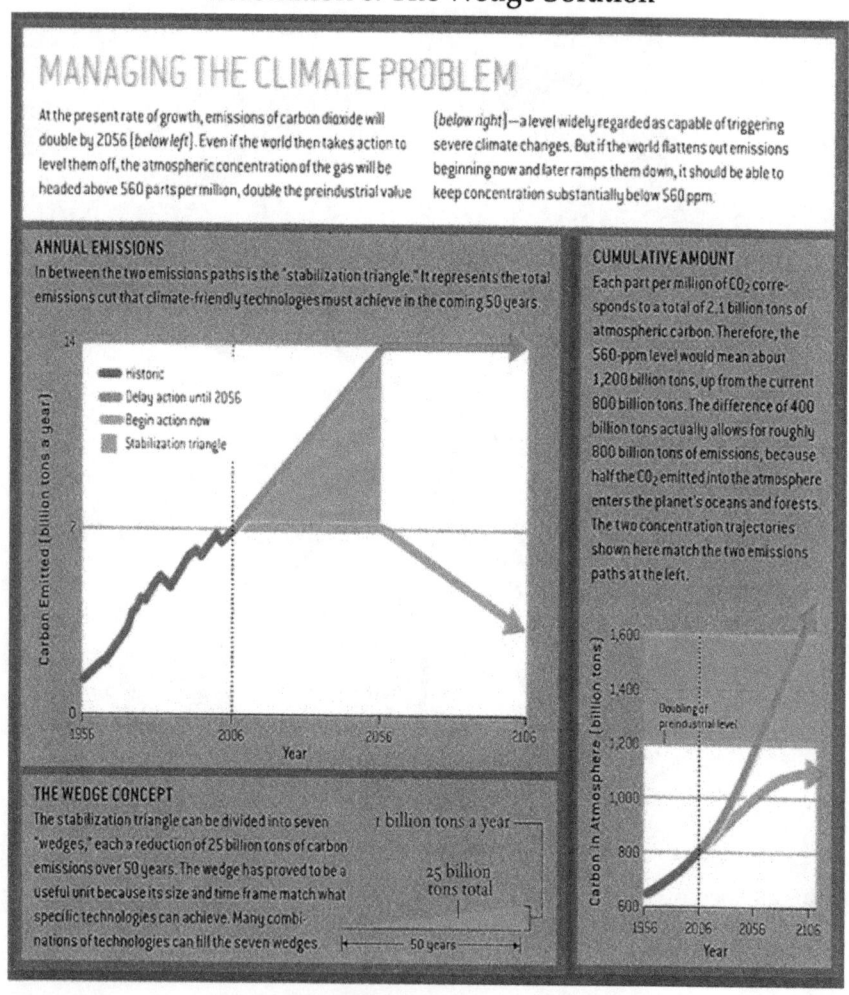

Source: Socolow and Pacala, 2004

(Mui et al 2007, 2-3), as can be seen in Illustration 7, on the following page.

This analysis provides a metric to make evaluations based on cumulative emission reductions over longer timeframes rather than incremental reductions for a specific year which are of primary significance in measuring impacts on global climate change.

The Role of Automotive Technology

The contribution of passenger vehicles to emissions reduction and flattening cannot be achieved without significant technological change. The real progress towards emissions reduction and flattening can only be achieved by new technologies which both reduce emissions and the amount of fuel used over the complete cycle. The table below illustrates that advanced technology to enhance present vehicles with gasoline and diesel engines can yield reductions in consumption of up to 40 percent and reduction of GHG emissions of up to 26 percent. Substantial progress towards flattening can only be achieved by technologies which lead both to improved fuel economy and a reduction in GHG emissions (Mui et al 2007, 13) as shown in Table 4.

The confounding aspect which we now face is that all of these technologies have been in development for at least some twenty

Table 4. Vehicle Technologies and Assumed Fuel Economy and GHG Emissions Relative to a Baseline Conventional Gasoline

Vehicle Technology	Vehicle Fuel Economy Improvement	Percent Reduction in GHG Emissions (fuel cycle)
	vs. Conventional Gasoline (Otto) Vehicle	
Advanced Gasoline and Diesel Engine	35-40%	20-26%
Hybrid Electric Vehicle (Gasoline)	40%	29%
Hybrid electric vehicle (Diesel)	70%	35%
Optimized E85 (ethanol based fuel)	-4%	30-80%
Advanced Optimized E85	30%	54-85%
Plug-In Hybrid electric	65%	31-62%
Electric	390%	31-94%
Fuel Cell	270%	21-92%

Source: Mui et al 2007

Illustration 7. U.S. Transportation Wedge Solution – Reduction of CO_2 Emission

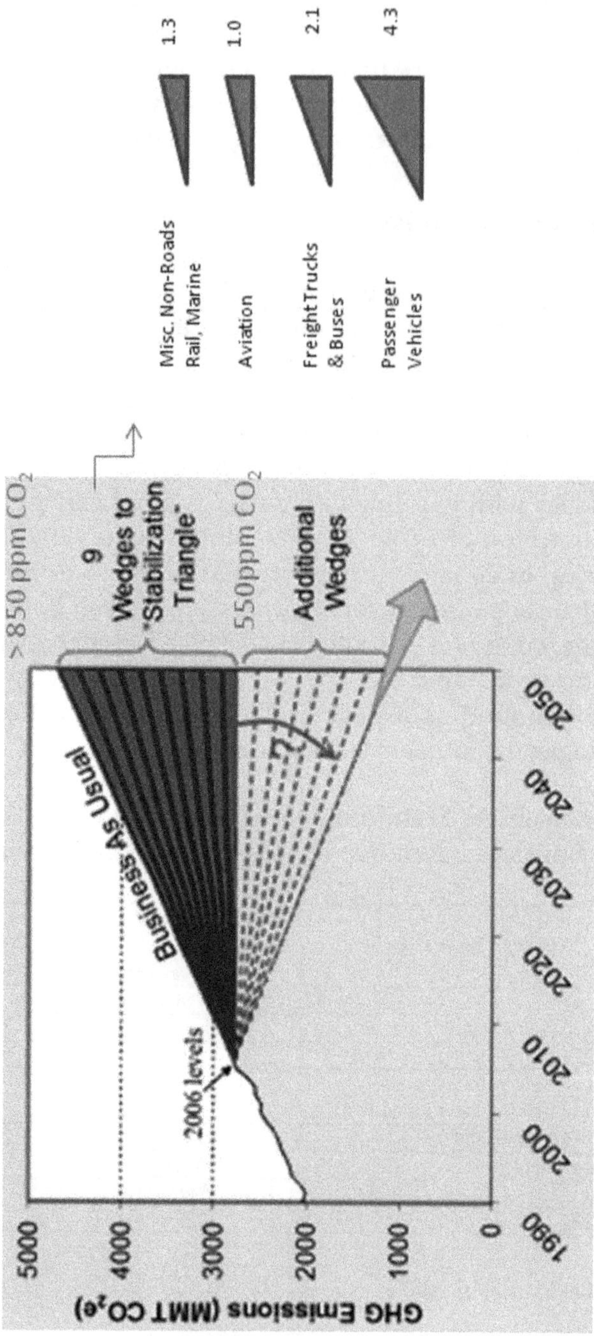

Source: Mui et al 2007

years, and some for more than a century. The remainder of this chapter will provide a brief review of some of these major developments. This discussion is intended to be neither exhaustive nor all-inclusive. Rather, it is intended to provide an overview of the present state of automotive technology with a focus on the U.S. passenger car sector to serve as a basis for the discussion in the following chapters.

According to a recent Pew study, the trend of rapidly rising CO_2 emissions "could be reversed. Light-duty vehicle fuel economy could be increased by one-fourth to one-third at less than the cost of the fuel saved over the vehicle's lifetime. Depending on technological progress, fuel economy could be increased by 50 to 100 percent by 2030. In the near term, improvements in engines and transmissions and in the reduction of aerodynamic drag, rolling resistance and vehicle weight could be implemented without compromising safety, handling, or comfort. In the long term, advanced diesel engines, gasoline or diesel hybrids and hydrogen powered fuel cell vehicles can yield more dramatic improvements" (Pew 2010).

The main barriers to the introduction and adaptation of new fuel efficient technologies are the low cost of gasoline in the U.S., the cost of implementing alternative technologies, and consumer acceptance. In the U.S., fuel for internal combustion gasoline powered engines is not only relatively inexpensive but is also "plentiful and energy-rich compared to current alternatives" (Kranz 2010a, 20J). A recent survey of global gasoline per gallon prices showed that the U.S. average price per gallon in the summer of 2010 at $2.72 per gallon of unleaded regular is $1.43 less than the world average of $4.15, a difference of 34.4 percent (Lewis 2010).

According to the *Automotive News*, automakers are still attempting to make gasoline engines more efficient for two reasons - to mitigate costs of implementing alternative and more efficient solutions and to retain the driving experience to which Americans are accustomed (Kranz 2010b, 20J). The presently pervasive gasoline-powered internal combustion engine has not been without limited competition over the years, but has prevailed as the leading technology and may well remain so. The reason for its undying popularity is simple and a function of our fellow countrymen's love of big and heavy SUVs and the sunk investments of automobile manufacturers in this technology. The main challenge is to glean more miles per gallon by reducing energy loss. Roughly 60 percent of energy loss is due to engine and exhaust heat, 15-25 percent due to deceleration and idling, 10-15 percent due to traction (roll resistance), and 5-10 percent due to drive train accessories. The remaining energy loss results from compensation to overcome vehicle weight and aerodynamic drag (Kranz 2010b, 20J).

Cost and consumer preferences are important factors leading automobile producers' decisions as the industry attempts to retain this technology despite the fact that even a change to more efficient fuels, such as ethanol E85 and optimized E85, as illustrated in Table 4, could lead to improved emissions reduction. Steve Ellis, manager of alternative-fuel vehicle sales and marketing at American Honda Motor Company, as quoted in *Automotive News*, estimates that even if, "tomorrow there is some magic bullet, 100 percent of every vehicle sold was not internal combustion, you would still have internal combustion engines out there for the next 20, 25 years" (Kranz 2010b, 20J).

There are some technological barriers that also need to be addressed. However, many of the alternative energy technologies have in existence for over a century and the technological barriers remain high due to the very fact that the development of these was shelved in deference to the automobile producers' and consumers' preference for the cost effective internal combustion engine which has become cost effective for three reasons – the relatively low cost of source fuel (petroleum), mass production to achieve scale effects of high profitability thereby reducing cost to the consumer, and efforts to achieve maximum profit on the enormous sunk cost of the capital investments required for vehicle and engine production and the cost of research and engineering development. Two alternative engine technologies, specifically electric engines and fuel cells, will be discussed here briefly to provide the background for the ensuing discussion in the following chapter.

The attempt to electrify vehicles began more than a century ago, both in the U.S. and in Europe. The American Electric Vehicle Company in Chicago, which was founded by the Massachusetts Institute of Technology graduate Clinton Edgar Woods in 1896, introduced a car with bearing driven axles and twin motor chain drives on the rear wheels. At the same time, the Columbia Motor Carriage Company of Hartford, Connecticut, touted as the first viable personal electric motor car company, designed and produced some 500 electric and 40 gasoline powered cars. In 1912, the Church-Field Motor Company of Sibley, Michigan produced a ten speed electric motor car with a two speed planetary gearbox and a Philco battery on a 100 inch chassis. The company offered two models, the two passenger Torpedo and the five passenger Coupe for the prices of $2,300 and $2,800, respectively. Henry Ford, founder of the Ford Motor Company collaborated with Thomas Edison on the development of electric vehicles in the period from 1913-1914 and actually built some prototypes. However, it was reported that he (Ford) preferred the performance of his tractors and "the shift to a war economy" which was vastly more profitable than the non-military business (Early Electric Car Site 2010).

In Europe, Ferdinand Porsche, founder of Porsche and the development engineer of the original Volkswagen, worked with Jacob Lohner in Vienna to design the Lohner-Porsche which debuted in 1900 at the Paris World Fair and featured wheels which were driven by electric hubs. The hybrid vehicle relied on batteries and a generator to produce electricity for the motors which were capable of speeds of 35 miles per hour (Economist 2010a, 78-79). Dubbed the *Mixte* (in English, mixed), the car's gasoline-fed engine which rotated at constant speed to drive the dynamo which charged a bank of accumulators which fed current to the hubs. This eliminated the need for drive shaft, transmission, chains, and a clutch. This simplified transmission operated with diminished loss of mechanical friction, as discussed above, and operated at an energy yield of 83 percent (Hybrid Vehicle Organization 2010).

Like electric motor technology, fuel cell technology is emerging as an alternative to gasoline and diesel powered engines and also has been in development for over a century. According to the Society of Automotive Engineers (SAE), in 1839, Sir William Grove discovered the possibility of generating electricity by reversing the electrolysis of water. Fifty years later, in 1889, Charles Langer and Ludwig Mond attempted to develop the first practical fuel cell using air and coal gasoline and coined the term "fuel cell". "While further attempts were made in the early 1900s to develop fuel cells that could convert coal or carbon into electricity, the advent of the internal combustion engine temporarily quashed any hopes of further development of the fledgling technology" (SAE 2011b).

Francis Bacon developed what was perhaps the first successful fuel cell device in 1932, with a hydrogen-oxygen cell using alkaline electrolytes and nickel electrodes, inexpensive alternatives to the catalysts used by Mond and Langer. Due to a substantial number of technical hurdles, it was not until 1959 that Bacon et al first demonstrated a practical five-kilowatt fuel cell system. Harry Karl Ihrig presented his now-famous 20-horsepower fuel cell-powered tractor that same year. In more recent decades, a number of manufacturers - including major auto makers - and various federal agencies have supported ongoing research into the development of fuel cell technology for use in fuel cell vehicles (FCV) and other applications. "Fuel cell energy is now expected to replace traditional power sources in coming years - from micro fuel cells to be used in cell phones to high-powered fuel cells for stock car racing" (SAE 2011b).

According to the *Automotive News*, fuel cells offer substantial benefits over internal combustion engines: twice the fuel efficiency, comparable precious metal-content, comparable durability, range, and performance, 60 percent fewer parts, 90 percent fewer moving parts, zero emissions and petroleum use, cold and hot weather capability, fast refueling" (Kranz 2010b, 20H). Given that fuel cell powered vehicles offer range, performance, and refueling comparable to gasoline-powered vehicles, these vehicles also may well be superior in consumer acceptance to electric vehicles.

This review of climate change, as related to the U.S. passenger car sector, and examples of available technology provides the basis for the further discussion. Namely, if we have, with a high degree of certitude, recognized that we are faced with an environmental problem which may present a major threat to human life and that we can to identifiable degrees control this through available automotive technology, why we have not chosen to do so with concerted action.

III.

The U.S. Passenger Car System

The promotion and adaptation of such new technologies to mitigate the effects of climate change through the reduction and flattening of CO_2 emissions from passenger cars will require intense cooperation among the participants in the U.S. passenger car sector. I define these as the oil industry, the government, the automobile producers, and the consumer. I will investigate the major motivational and situational forces within each of these groups and those shared between one or more of them via a historical analysis of the development of the relationships between the participant groups of the passenger car sector. I will show how these forces increasingly make cooperation, at best, difficult and may even polarize cooperative efforts and that each of these groups increasingly acts as an independent agent driven by common forces with conflicting dimensions. By showing that each of these participant groups is an interacting agent with the other groups, it can be argued that this sector is a system, according to the definition proposed by Miller and Page, a composition of interacting and thinking agents (Miller and Page 2007, 3). The relationships between the groups are neither clear-cut nor well defined and these have grown and changed over time. The evolving pattern reflects a decrease in centralized control by the oil industry, the government, and the automobile producers who have historically, both individually and collectively, exerted control over the sector, representing a transformation to emergent and ever increasing independent action.

In order to reduce emission from the passenger vehicle sector, new technologies such as those introduced in Chapter II will have to be deployed. This will require substantial cash investment in research and development activities to engineer viable technological solutions for vehicle propulsion as well as substantial capital investment in new manufacturing facilities and processes to produce these new technologies. The cost of these new products will be passed on to and increase the burden on the consumer. The consumer will be confronted with the choice between maintaining the status quo of contributing to climbing CO_2 emissions by purchasing vehicles without these new technologies, higher investment costs for a vehicle equipped with new technology which either substantially reduces or does not contribute to these emissions, or a change in behavior to rely on public transportation, which in many areas in the U.S. is not readily available and thus may not represent a viable option for many consumers. The problem is further compounded by the socio-economic distribution of wealth in this country.

Rural Americans are, on the average, poorer than urban Americans and they rely more on fossil fuels. (The term American, as used in this thesis, refers exclusively to U.S. Americans). Rural Americans are dependent on gasoline-guzzling, emission-billowing farm and land equipment for their living. They generally have to rely on a car to drive to stores to purchase goods and services and for participation in social activities. Rising oil prices impact the rural poor twofold. The price of fuel for personal transportation rises. At the same time, rising fuel prices lead to an increase in transportation costs which impact the prices of those commodities upon which rural Americans depend for their livelihood, i.e. grain, fertilizer and pesticides (Economist 2009, 44).

As the economic situation in the U.S. worsens, concern regarding environmental issues is declining. According to a recent Gallup poll for the first time in its 25-year history of asking Americans about the trade-off between environmental protection and economic growth, a majority of Americans say economic growth should be given the priority, even if the environment suffers to some extent (Illustration 8, p. 29)..

These facts highlight the focus of the U.S. passenger car sector on economic benefit measured by cost, which may be the only common underlying motivational factor among the participant groups.

**Illustration 8. Results of Gallup Poll:
The Economy vs. The Environment**

With which one of these statements about the environment and the economy do you most agree — [ROTATED: protection of the environment should be given priority, even at the risk of curbing economic growth (or) economic growth should be given priority, even if the environment suffers to some extent]?

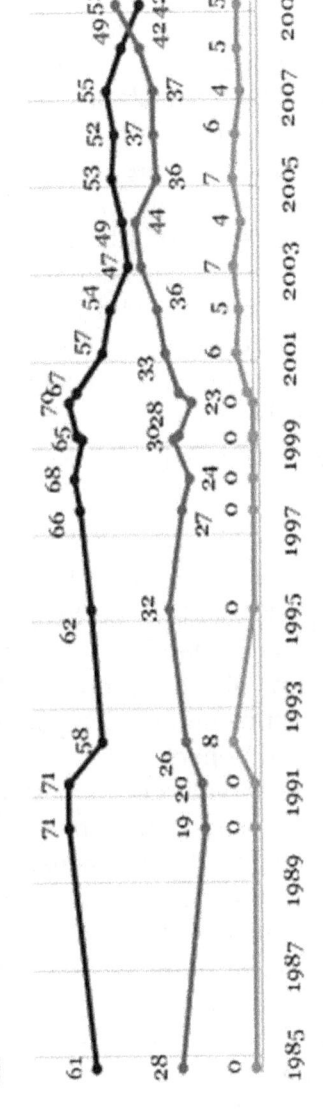

(vol.) = Volunteered response

GALLUP POLL

Source: Newport 2009

When confronted with decisions regarding a choice of automotive-related technology which could contribute to reduction and flattening of CO_2 emissions, all participant groups tend to weigh these decisions as cost-benefit analyses. As previously noted, according to Sagoff, "It is the characteristic of cost-benefit analysis that it treats all value judgments other than those made on its behalf as nothing but statements of preference, attitude, or emotion, insofar as they are value judgments. The cost-benefit analyst regards as true the judgments that we should maximize efficiency or wealth" (Sagoff 1998, 331). He maintains that we tend to want to reduce all decisions to a type of data-based decision or a cost-benefit analysis (Sagoff 1998, 328). The following portion of this chapter will examine the underlying facts and motivational and situational forces influencing the cost/benefit decision-making processes within each participant group in the U.S. passenger car sector, as defined above.

The Oil Industry

The relationship between the oil industry and the other U.S. passenger car sector participants, in particular, certain automobile producers, has existed since the 1900s and is characterized by intimate and intricate patterns of interaction. In addition to strong historical linkages between certain oil companies and some automobile producers, a key component of this complex matrix of interplay involves the government at municipal, state, and the federal levels. The common denominator which links these three parties is automotive demand, driven by cost/benefit factors. This portion of Chapter III will discuss some relevant highlights of such relationships. The three factors which will be considered in this section are the relation between oil industry and the automobile producers, their relationships with the government, and the cost of petroleum. This discussion is not intended to portray the oil industry, the automobile producers, or particular firms as the bad guys. As has been discussed in the previous chapter, consumer behavior drives the market and the U.S. consumers' preference for large, heavy, fuel-inefficient cars must also be kept in mind. However, the oil industry's continued focus on the profitable production of petroleum is a major factor contributing to the proliferation of gasoline powered engines and the rise in CO_2 emissions in the U.S.

Three aspects will be considered in this discussion: the historical intimate relation between certain automobile producers and oil companies using the example of General Motors and E.I. du Pont de Nemours & Co. (Du Pont), whereby it must be noted that this discussion is not intended to position either General Motors or Du Pont as the sole instigators of efforts to circumvent the propagation of alternative fuels, but rather to highlight the intertwined historical facets of the oil industry's relationship with the automobile producers and the interest of both industries to continue to profit from the growth of existing technologies, i.e. the production of petroleum-based fuel and the proliferation of the gasoline-powered internal combustion engine, to increase revenue and profit and grow their respective businesses. Most automobile producers have been involved in struggles with legislation aimed at restricting or inhibiting the use of gasoline- powered internal combustion engines. Second, the relation of the U.S. government to the oil industry and automobile producers with regard to passenger cars will be reviewed, and thirdly, the cost/profit aspect.

The relation between the oil industry and automobile producers has two facets. The first is the development of automotive fuels and the second is the aspect of common corporate ownership and initiatives. Two aspects regarding automotive fuel development in the U.S. will be used to illustrate these facets - that of lead-based gasoline and also alternative fuels and technologies which reduce CO_2 emissions from passenger cars, which is the main topic of this thesis. The leaded gasoline discussion is relevant because it succinctly highlights the concerted interaction and cooperation between certain members of the oil and automobile industries in the past.

It has been known for centuries that chemical lead is poisonous and detrimental to human health. The first evidence of this was discovered around 100 B.C. (Kitman 2000). Diagnoses of lead poisoning in the U.S. were reported in the late 1800s. In the early 1900s, France, Austria, and Belgium issued the first bans on lead-based paints (Kitman 2000).

In 1916, United Motors and General Motors purchased Dayton Engineering Laboratories Company, later known as DELCO, from Charles Kettering. Kettering was investigating the use of lead additives to gasoline to prevent engine knock in gasoline-powered engines in passenger cars (Kitman 2000). DELCO "became the foundation for the General Motors Research Corporation of which Kettering became vice president in 1920" (Scharchburg 2011). Two key developments followed shortly thereafter. According to Kitman, in 1918 the *Scientific American* reported that an alcohol blend gasoline, which was an early alternative fuel, was suitable for use in vehicle motors. That same year, he reports, Thomas Midgley patented a benzene-gasoline blend as an antiknock agent. Shortly thereafter, Du Pont increased its share in General Motors and, by the year 1920, owned 35 percent of General Motors (Kitman 2000).

The relationship between Du Pont and General Motors, characterized by joint efforts for the development of automotive fuels and inter-corporate ownership, grew rapidly thereafter. In 1921, Midgley discovered that the addition of tetraethyl lead (TEL) to gasoline could also curb engine knock in gasoline powered internal combustion engines. The following year, General Motors contracted Du Pont to supply TEL. Although scientific concerns regarding the health effects of TEL were raised and Midgley, himself, suffered from the effects of lead poisoning, General Motors established General Motors Chemical Corporation to produce TEL, and leaded gasoline became available in the U.S. Standard Oil, which was founded in 1870 by John D. Rockefeller (Public Broadcasting Service 2011), began the production of TEL in 1924 and in that same year, together with General Motors, formed Ethyl Gasoline Corporation. Following conflicting reports by some public officials in 1924, General Motors, Standard Oil, and Du Pont requested the U.S. Surgeon General to hold public hearings regarding the use of TEL in automotive fuel. Four years later, after several more TEL plants had been opened, the Lead Industries Association was formed to "combat undesirable publicity". At the same time, the Surgeon General announced in New York that it found no grounds to ban TEL (Kitman 2000).

In 1930, the Ethyl Gasoline Corporation established a new company in England, Ethyl Export, to handle non U.S. domestic business (Global Lead Network 2011 and Kitman 2000). Subsidiaries were founded in Italy, France, and Germany, and in 1938 Ethyl Export became the Associated Ethyl Company. According to the Global Lead Network, "the company was formed to control TEL production throughout Britain and France, and its primary goal was to expand the use of TEL, which it did by the clever and expedient of making shareholders out of six leading oil companies - BP, Shell, Esso (as Standard Oil of New Jersey was known in England), Mobil, Chevron and Texaco - as well as General Motors" (Global Lead Network 2011).

In 1949, the U.S. Justice Department filed an antitrust suit against Du Pont to, according to Kitman, "break up the largest single concentration of power in the United States". The main target, Kitman maintains, was DuPont's multi- million dollar investment in General Motors. The suit focused on the "anticompetitive association between it [Du Pont], General Motors, Standard Oil, and Ethyl" (Kitman 2000). Five years later, the suit was dismissed in Chicago's U.S. District Court by Judge Walter J. LaBuy, who, according to *Time Magazine*, after studying over 2,000 exhibits and 8,283 pages of testimony ruled that, "The government has failed to prove conspiracy, monopolization, a restraint of trade, or any probability of a restraint." *Time* further notes that an appeal to the Supreme Court for a reversal was not successful and that La Buy's decision "seemed foolproof and final" (*Time* 1957).

By mid-1957, DuPont controlled 23 percent of General Motors and even though its ownership percentage was diluted from the previously cited 35 percent due to changes in investors and investments, Du Pont was still the largest shareholder. The stake was worth approximately $2.7 billion dollars. In addition to the jointly held fuel development activities, General Motors and Du Pont had entered into agreements whereby DuPont would supply certain products for vehicles produced by General Motors.

In 1957, a surprise ruling by the U.S. Supreme Court overturned the LaBuy decision, "bypassing the Government's main charges - that Du Pont had violated the 1890 Sherman Act by fencing off the General Motors market from Du Pont's competitors" and based its opinion on Section 7 of the Clayton Act which prohibited corporations from acquiring stock, directly or indirectly, of another corporation with the effect of lessening competition, restraining commerce, or creating the tendency to create a monopoly (Walkley and Zimmerman 1958, 266).

In 1961, the Europe-based Associated Ethyl changed its name to

Associated Octel Company Limited, "reflecting the fact that Ethyl and Octel were now competitors for European and Latin American business. In 1962, Ethyl was sold by General Motors and Standard Oil to the Gottwald family of Richmond, Virginia, owners of Albemarle Paper" (Global Lead Network 2011) in a leveraged buyout for $200 million which was "partially financed by the sellers, General Motors and Standard Oil" (Kitman 2000). Today, after a series of further sales and takeovers, Octel is a member of Innospec Inc., an international specialty chemicals company which employs over 850 people in 20 countries and has an annual sales volume of approximately $600 million. Innospec's business covers three areas: Fuel Specialties, Active Chemicals and Octane Additives and the company is listed on the NASDAQ as IOSP. As noted on the company's website, "Two years ago our company went through a major transformation programme and we changed our name to Innospec to reflect our new strategic direction as a multi-product specialty chemicals business. However, we can trace our origins back almost 70 years to the days of the Associated Ethyl Company Limited, which later became Associated Octel". As also noted on the website, "Our Octane Additives business is the world's only producer of tetraethyl lead (TEL), an octane enhancer used in automotive gasoline for vehicles that run on leaded fuel" (Innospec 2011).

Through the early 1990s, lead was still being used as an additive to gasoline to reduce engine knock in high compression engines to avoid having to use higher octane gasoline, which was more expensive and would increase the cost of ownership to the consumer. As reported by Bridbord and Hanson, there exist solid evidence that "the oil and lead industries used various strategies to forestall regulation of lead in gasoline" and that these industries, along with manufacturers of gasoline additives, had "successfully thwarted government efforts to limit lead in gasoline for 50 years" (Bridbord and Hanson 2009, 1195).

In 1970, automobiles in the U.S were emitting 200,000 tons of lead per annum, mainly in urban areas (Bridbord and Hanson 2009, 1195). In 1973, the EPA issued the U.S. EPA 1973d Health-Based Lead Phase-Down Regulation Limits on Allowable Levels of Lead in Gasoline which established the target for the maximum allowable led level in gasoline of 1.7 grams lead per gallon of gasoline after January 1975, decreasing to 0.5 g lead/gallon of gasoline after January 1979 (Bridbord and Hanson 2009, 1200). The initial challenge to this ruling in the U.S. Court of Appeals on September 9, 1974 was the case Ethyl Corp. v. U.S. EPA, resulting in the regulation being set aside on January 25, 1975. The regulation was affirmed in a subsequent appeal on March 19, 1976 (Ethyl Corp. v. U.S. EPA 1976). Due to the fact that the U.S. Supreme Court decided not to agree to hear an appeal of the decision, the regulation took effect in 1976, three years after it had been issued by the EPA (Bridbord and Hanson 2009, 1199).

By 1995, lead emissions had been reduced to 2,000 tons per year, down from 200,000 tons in 1970 (Bridbord and Hanson 2009, 1195). In the beginning of 1996, the EPA issued a final rulemaking and the Clean Air Act banned the sale of leaded fuel for use in on-road vehicles in the U.S. The EPA ruled that fuel containing lead may continue to be sold for off-road uses, including aircraft, racing cars, farm equipment, and marine engines (EPA 1996). Although the EPA press release hailed the ruling as a "mark to the end of a quarter-of-a-century of work to keep Americans safe from exposure to lead", it also noted the elimination of certain requirements for gasoline refiners and importers as well as for automobile producers which would help to reduce compliance costs for the industry (EPA 1996).

It is clear, from the above discussion, that the interests of the oil industry were tied to the growth of the automotive industry and the proliferation of the gasoline-powered combustion engine which, in turn, contributed to increasing CO_2 emissions. It can also be seen that these efforts may well have been directly or indirectly enhanced by governmental actions. According to Ian Rutledge in *Addicted to Oil*, at the beginning of the twentieth century only 12 percent of all refined U.S. petroleum was used in gasoline and the first drive-in gasoline station opened in 1907. By the 1929/1930 period, 44.8 percent of all U.S. petroleum was used for gasoline and the number of drive-in gasoline stations had increased to 143,000. Between 1920 and 1930, gasoline consumption increased from 101 million barrels per annum to 394.8 million barrels per annum. The rapid rise in gasoline demand led to a "doubling of domestic crude oil production over the same period". Rutledge explains that the production of crude oil did not increase in proportion to the rise in gasoline demand due to improved refining techniques which increased the proportion of gasoline in total refined products (Rutledge 2006, 15).

In addition, two trends occurred, which Rutledge maintains further intensified the common interest of the U.S. oil and automobile industries and were supported by the U.S. government - the urbanization of the U.S. and the need to fuel the economic recovery after the Great Depression of the 1930s. Prior to that time, the principal demand for automobiles came from customers living in rural areas. From 1910 to 1930, the percent of the U.S. population living in urban areas rose from 45.7 percent to 56.2 percent. This trend impacted sales of cars as reflected in a statement by Paul Hoffman, the President of Studebaker, in 1934, "Sales resistance to further absorption comes from the inability to use automobiles effectively rather than from inability to own them." The urban well-to-do, he maintained, "will tell you, the ownership lacks advantage. They can use mass transportation more conveniently for many of their movements" (Hoffman 1939, 4).

According to Rutledge, a planned strategic elimination of public transportation, beginning with electric street cars and replacement of these with gasoline and later, diesel- fueled motor buses, was undertaken. This was followed by a reduction in bus service, leading to the motorization of urban America. He maintains that the decline in street car use, as evidenced by a 46 percent decline in carried passengers from 1923 to 1942 and an increase of passengers carried by motorbuses of over 900 percent in the same period was not due to consumer preference, but rather, due to the concerted effort of General Motors and several oil companies with support of the U.S. government, which allowed the formation of several companies jointly owned by General Motors and the oil companies to dismantle the streetcar industry across the U.S. He states, that "in 1936 National City Lines was established through an amalgamation of a number of smaller motor bus companies in which General Motors had equity, or whose management was controlled by General Motors through interlocking directorships. Then National City Lines' stock was sold to General Motors, itself, to Chevron, and to Phillips Petroleum. Two years later, Pacific City Lines, another transit-acquiring company, was set up by General Motors and Chevron" (Rutledge 2006, 16).

Rutledge continues to report on this joint effort. He maintains that, "the destruction of efficient and profitable public transportation by General Motors/Chevron front companies was carried out most thoroughly and ruthlessly in California between 1946 and 1958", during which time the electric streetcar and light rail systems of the municipalities of East Bay, San Jose, Fresno, Sacramento, and San Diego were purchased by either Pacific City Lines or National City Lines and were then subsequently closed (Rutledge 2006, 17). He further notes that, despite evidence of widespread public opposition and efforts to block the sales and closures by local city councils, the closures were effected. Rutledge maintains that, thereafter a "downward spiral of decline" set in, characterized by reduced service leading to higher fares, which put pressure on people to buy cars. He notes that by 1940, approximately one-tenth of the U.S. population, at that time, had no access to public transportation (Rutledge 2006, 17).

Although I could not find reference to Bradford Snell, widely considered as the father of the General Motors conspiracy theory, in *Addicted to Oil*, Rutledge is, in essence, reconfirming and embellishing Snell's conspiracy theory. In 1974, as reported by Cliff Slater in "General Motors and the Demise of the Street Car", Snell, an antitrust attorney for the U.S. Senate, testified before the Senate Subcommittee on Antitrust and Monopoly. His testimony stated that the government had brought criminal charges against General Motors and allied parties for their involvement in the destruction of one hundred electric rail systems throughout the U.S. Snell further testified that this corporate constellation was, in actuality, a conspiracy to replace electric transportation with either gasoline or diesel powered buses with the result that millions of Americans were left without an alternative to travel by car (Slater 1997, 45-46).

Slater maintains that Snell's allegations are a myth, and that, although General Motors was convicted of "conspiring with others in the automotive industry to monopolize the sale of supplies used by local transportation companies controlled by the City Lines defendants....This is a far cry from conspiring to wreck economically viable transit systems" (Slater 1997, 47). According to Slater, what really led to the rise of the motor bus and replacement of electric street cars was the jitney, which he views as the precursor to the motor bus. He suggests that the industry simply misjudged the importance of this mode of passenger transportation as a prelude to the demise of the electric street car and emergence of the motor bus (Slater 1997, 49).

The first jitneys were introduced in 1914 in Los Angeles. These vehicles were regular gasoline-powered automobiles which carried passengers along a fixed route. The fare which was a nickel, bore the slang name jitney, and hence the name of the mode of transportation. By 1915, jitneys as passenger transportation vehicles, reached a peak of 62,000 vehicles in service, nationally. This rapid rise had a major impact on streetcar usage and some streetcar companies experienced reduced ridership of up to 50 percent. According to Slater, streetcar companies persuaded local and state governments to introduce legislation to significantly reduce the advantages enjoyed by jitney operators. Regulations were imposed which severely limited the operation and profitability of the jitneys. These included a requirement of liability bonds and the provision of free transportation to city employees, as well as restriction of route length and travel speed, the limitation of jitney operation to certain days and low-ridership areas, and the prohibition of curbside waiting. As a result, only about 6,000 jitneys were in use by the end of 1916 (Slater 1997, 48-49).

David St. Clair presents, perhaps, the most neutral and informed review of the alleged conspiracy in *The Motorization of American Cities*. He provides a detailed description of the acquisition strategy pursued by General Motors et al, confirming Rutledge's depiction of these actions, but also delves into the economics of the situation. St. Clair dissects Snell's argument that the sale of a single General Motors motor bus at the price of $40,000 would result in a loss of over $466,200 due to lost car sales because people would not buy cars. Snell's argument was based on the assumption that a single bus could replace 35 cars, based on an average price of $3,700 per car and an average life span of 5 years for a car versus 18 years for a bus, resulting in a loss to General Motors of some $466,200 in lost car sales (St Clair 1986, 76). St. Clair refutes Snell's assumptions by correctly stating that, although General Motors' automotive operations were its most profitable, "there is no reason to suppose that some of those 35 cars would not have been sold anyway, even if 35 customers used public transportation....The 35 lost sales is therefore too high and confuses the bus's capacity to carry 35 commuters with lost automotive sales" (St. Clair 1986, 76).

St. Clair also presents detailed macroeconomic analyses and comparisons of the profitability of the bus, trolley coach, and street car industries. He shows that the average profit in terms of cent per mile from 1936 - 1950 was 3.9 cents for buses, 15.3 cents for new trolley coaches, and 6.8 cents for street cars (St. Clair 1986, 51). His analysis of rate of returns, based on annual mileage with equal service, shows a 2.2 percent return for the motor bus and 15.0 percent for trolley coaches (St. Clair 1986, 52). He notes that these analyses make a strong case for the economic superiority of the trolley coach and the street car to the motor bus during the period analyzed, but also that this does not necessarily validate the conspiracy argument (St. Clair 1986, 53). However, St. Clair arrives at the conclusion that the evidence does support the allegation:

> One must conclude that the alternative explanations of the intent of the motorizers are weak. The activities of those alleged to have conspired to motorize and destroy public transit reveal a pattern that, when considered in the light of the preceding economic analysis, is highly suspect, to say the least. It must be stated that knowledge of these events is still incomplete, and that there is no "smoking gun". There is, however, a growing body of evidence that, taken as a whole, does strongly support the allegation. (St. Clair 1986, 77)

Jones, in line with St. Clair, concurs with the description of the situation surrounding the antitrust case against General Motors. He notes that the company Hertz, originally in the taxi business, was also linked to National City Lines and that the acquisitions of that company were financed almost exclusively by General Motors and Firestone Tire and Rubber and "through other National City Line subsidiaries to Phillips Petroleum, Standard Oil of California and Mack Manufacturing Corporation". Jones maintains that the General Motors antitrust case, which was finally settled in 1947, when General Motors signed a consent decree which curtailed its involvement in transit operations, came at a time when "large injections of capital were needed to replace the worn-out fleet of transit vehicles that had limped through the peak ridership of World War II, an application of federal statutes had once again deprived transit of a source of funds" (Jones 2008, 62-63).

Thus far, it has been shown that the oil and automotive industries in the U.S. have historically shared a common interest to promote gasoline-powered passenger vehicles.This may well have contributed to, if not had driven, an increase in passenger car sales and a corresponding increase fuel consumption, leading to increasing emissions of CO_2 from passenger vehicles in the U.S. It has also been shown that the government has not, in all cases and at all times, been a stalwart watchdog and regulator, but has, at times, supported the efforts of the oil and automotive industries to achieve these goals by either not acting on matters in a timely fashion, as illustrated by the case of the regulation of lead-based gasoline and the EPA phase out of lead-based fuel for on-road vehicles or through the decisions which would have broken cartel-like relationships, such as the General Motors/Du Pont case, which was only resolved several years after the initial ruling.

The third factor, which is key to understanding the role of the oil industry as a major participant in the U.S. passenger car sector, is the economic factor. This can be viewed in terms of fuel pricing, as well as operative cost reduction to maintain and increase profitability. The following will provide a brief overview of both of these economic determinants, relative to the oil industry.

Economics play a particular role in the U.S. oil industry. As noted by the U.S. Energy Information Administration (EIA), the U.S, once the leading global producer of oil and now the second rank, is not only the oldest major global producer of oil but also the world's largest importer, and has produced more oil, cumulatively, than any other country (180 billion barrels from 1918 to 1999) and more oil, cumulatively, than the present reserves of any country, with the exception of Saudi Arabia (EIA 2011b). In 1994, the demand for crude oil exceeded domestic production and has been met, increasingly, by imported crude oil (EIA 1997, 49). An analysis of the EIA report on crude oil highlights for November 2010 released on January 28, 2011, depicted in the following Table 5, shows that three

Table 5. U.S. Crude Oil Imports - Top 15 Countries 2009 and 2010 in Thousand Barrels/Day

Country	Nov. 2010 Tsd. Barrels/Day	Nov. 2010 % Total Top 15 Imports	YTD 2010 Tsd. Barrels/Day	YTD 2010 % Total Top 15 Imports	YTD 2009 Tsd. Barrels/Day	YTD 2009 % Total Top 15 Imports	% Change YTD 2010 2009
Canada	1,975	23.9%	1,963	22.7%	1,928	23.4%	1.8%
Mexico	1,229	14.9%	1,132	13.1%	1,095	13.3%	3.3%
Saudi Arabia	1,119	13.6%	1,081	12.5%	991	12.0%	8.3%
Venezuela	884	10.7%	920	10.7%	968	11.8%	-5.2%
Nigeria	806	9.8%	982	11.4%	753	9.1%	23.3%
Colombia	489	5.9%	349	4.0%	258	3.1%	26.1%
Algeria	379	4.6%	331	3.8%	276	3.4%	16.6%
Iraq	340	4.1%	421	4.9%	461	5.6%	-9.5%
Angola	263	3.2%	387	4.5%	465	5.7%	-20.2%
Ecuador	188	2.3%	196	2.3%	190	2.3%	3.1%
Brazil	188	2.3%	252	2.9%	306	3.7%	-21.4%
Kuwait	170	2.1%	202	2.3%	182	2.2%	9.9%
Russia	85	1.0%	261	3.0%	236	2.9%	9.6%
United Kingdom	80	1.0%	120	1.4%	106	1.3%	11.7%
Indonesia	55	0.7%	34	0.4%	15	0.2%	55.9%
Total Top 15	8,250	100.0%	8,631	100.0%	8,230	100.0%	4.6%

Source: EIA 2011b

countries—Canada, Mexico, and Saudi Arabia—exported more than one thousand barrels daily to the U.S. in November 2010. The amount imported from the top fifteen importing countries rose almost 5 percent over the same period in 2009.

In addition, the production of crude oil in the U.S. has several unique factors in comparison to that in the rest of the world, which also contributes to the explanation of the particular focus of the U.S. oil industry on economics. Unlike in most other major oil producing countries where the government owns the rights to develop resources, in the U.S. this is a partially a matter of private ownership and the undertaking of exploration for and production of oil is a decision made between the landowner and the production company which compensates the landowner by means of a mutually agreed upon royalty based on dollars per barrel of oil produced. As the EIA notes, "early in the industry's development, there were few government restrictions. Now, there are overriding rules about well spacing and environmental standards. The only government agency to restrict production volumes was the Texas Railroad Commission, which limited production in Texas depending on demand and production volumes in other areas of the United States. However, since the early 1970s, there have been no restrictions to production by any government agency" (EIA 2011a).

The aspect of private ownership of resource rights in the U.S. allows for the active participation of independent producers and the dominant presence of stripper wells, those onshore wells which produce less than 10 barrels a day. Stripper wells account for 75 percent of all onshore wells in the U.S. and produce about 900,000 barrels a day, roughly 15 percent of U.S. daily crude oil production. Both of these aspects are unique to the production of oil in the U.S. They also provide an explanation of the broad participation in the U.S. oil production industry as entrepreneurs from both the production side as well as land owners joined forces to search for and produce crude oil (EIA 2011a) and make a profit while doing so.

Ownership of onshore wells and drilling facilities on government-owned land is managed by the U.S. Department of the Interior's Bureau of Land Management (BLM) which has responsibility for oil and gas leasing on some "564 million acres of BLM, national forest, and other Federal lands, as well as State and private surface lands where mineral rights have been retained by the Federal Government". Production from Federal onshore oil wells accounts for 5 percent of U.S. domestic crude oil production (Department of the Interior, Bureau of Land Management 2011).

The U.S. Department of the Interior's Bureau of Ocean Energy Management is responsible for the minerals management and leasing of offshore wells on the 1.7 billion acres of the Outer Continental Shelf. he Outer Continental Shelf (OCS) is defined by the U.S. Federal Government as, "the submerged lands, subsoil, and seabed, lying between the seaward extent of the State' jurisdiction and the seaward extent of Federal jurisdiction which is defined "as the furthest of 200 nautical miles seaward of the baseline from which the breadth of the territorial sea is measured or, if the continental shelf can be shown to exceed 200 nautical miles, a distance not greater than a line 100 nautical miles from the 2500 meter isobath or a line 350 nautical miles from the baseline". Certain states also have jurisdiction over adjacent areas, which is defined as follows: "Texas and the Gulf coast of Florida are extended three marine leagues (approximately 4.4 statute miles) seaward from the baseline from which the breadth of the territorial sea is measured. Louisiana is extended three imperial nautical miles (imperial nautical mile = 6080.2 feet) seaward of the baseline from which the breadth of the territorial sea is measured. All other States' seaward limits are extended three nautical miles (approximately 3.3 statute miles) seaward of the baseline from which the breadth of the territorial seaward is measured." The production of these offshore wells accounts for about 30 percent of the U.S. domestic oil production (U.S. Department of the Interior, Bureau of Ocean Energy Management 2011).

Crude oil prices measure the spot price of various oil types, most commonly either the West Texas Intermediate (WTI), which is light, sweet crude with a low sulfur content and is the crude of choice for gasoline production or Brent Blend. Sulfur, a nonmetallic, odorless, tasteless chemical element, insoluble in water, can exist as a gas, liquid, or solid. Sulfur is present in petroleum crudes and needs to be removed. Therefore, the higher the sulfur content, the more expensive the refining of the crude oil becomes. Hence, the WTI crude is preferred for the production of gasoline, as the refining costs are considerably lower than those of more sour crudes which have higher sulfur content (Amaden 2011).

Brent Blend is a combination of crude oil from 15 different oil fields in the North Sea and is primarily refined in Northwest Europe. Although it is less light and less sweet than WTI, it is still well-suited for making gasoline. The OPEC Basket Price, which OPEC uses to monitor world oil markets, is an average of the prices of oil from Algeria, Indonesia, Nigeria, Saudi Arabia, Dubai, Venezuela, and Mexico (Amaden 2011). OPEC, the Organization of the Petroleum Exporting Countries was founded in Iraq in 1960 with five original members, Iran, Iraq, Kuwait, Saudi Arabia, and Venezuela. Other countries joining thereafter included Qatar in 1961, Indonesia and Libya in1962, the United Arab Emirates in 1967, Algeria in 1969, Nigeria in 1971, Ecuador in 1973, Gabon in 1975 and Angola in 2007. Ecuador suspended its membership from December 1992 until October 2007, Gabon terminated its membership in 1995, and Indonesia suspended its membership in January, 2009 (OPEC 2011).

WTI is generally priced at about a $5-6 per barrel premium to the OPEC Basket Price and about $1-2 per-barrel premium to Brent. Brent blend is generally priced at about a $4 per barrel premium to the OPEC Basket price or about a $1-2 per barrel discount to WTI. OPEC prices are lower because the oil from some of the countries is more sour, having a higher sulfur content, and is therefore less suited to producing gasoline. The New York Mercantile Exchange (NYMEX) is the world's largest physical commodity futures exchange and is located in New York City. The NYMEX futures price for crude oil represents the value of 1,000 barrels of oil, usually WTI, at some agreed upon time in the future. However, the futures price usually follows the spot price closely, since the oil pricing is closely tied to threats to disruption of supply which cannot easily and with certainty be predicted in advance (Amaden 2011). The most recent events in Egypt give witness to this, as reported by Sampson in *Business Week*, "Oil prices hovered near $92 a barrel amid concerns over a power struggle in Egypt, which has been rocked by anti-government protests, could shut the Suez Canal – a major route for oil tankers to Europe and North America" (Sampson 2011).

Crude oil prices are determined by global supply and demand. On the demand side of the equation, world economic growth is the biggest factor. Growing economies require energy, and oil accounts for over 35% of the world's total energy consumption. On the supply side, perhaps the most tightly controlled source of oil is OPEC, an organization of twelve oil-producing countries formed in 1960 to regulate supply and, according to the EIA, "to some extent the price of oil". According to the EIA, the OPEC, recognizing that they were dealing with a non-renewable resource and that internal competition would drive prices higher and low pricing would lead to a more imminent depletion of their oil, "they set a goal to attempt to keep oil prices at about $70/barrel to maintain a balance as higher pricing could provide other countries the incentive to drill new fields which are too expensive to open when prices are low" (EIA 2011).

Higher crude oil prices directly affect the cost of gasoline, home heating oil, manufacturing, and electric power generation. According to the EIA, in the U.S., 96 percent of transportation relies on oil and 43 percent of industrial production, 21 percent of residential and commercial, and 3 percent of electric power are oil-dependent (EIA 2011). High oil prices, which increase the cost of transportation, affect virtually all aspects of consumption, especially fuel for cars and for the transportation of goods and food.

In the U.S., crude oil accounts for 55 percent of the price of gasoline, while distribution and taxes influence the remaining 45 percent. In June 2008, the price of WTI crude oil hit an all-time high of $145 per barrel. By December 2008, it had fallen to a low of $30 per barrel. The U.S. average retail price for a gallon of regular gasoline also hit a peak in July 2008 of $4.10, rising as high as $5 per gallon in some areas. By December 2008, in a move correlating with the price of oil, the price of gasoline had dropped to $1.68 per gallon (EIA 2010). As of February 12, 2011, the price of crude (WIT) has climbed to $85.58, down slightly from the beginning of the month when it traded at $88.92 (Shore and Kahn 2011) According to the Associated Press, the price of gasoline in the US "hit a record high for the time of year" on Friday, February 11, 2011 when the national average price for a gallon of gasoline was $3.127, "about 50 cents higher than a year ago" (Associated Press 2011, A12).

As Simpkins notes in *Money Morning*, "despite fallout from the Gulf oil spill, drilling and oil service companies made big waves in the waning months of 2010. And they're likely to carry that success through 2011 as higher oil prices and political gridlock keeps the profits pumping." He also notes that most oil industry analysts believe that oil prices will reach $100 per barrel for the first time since 2008 and that some estimate that oil prices will reach $150/barrel in 2011, climbing higher than the previous all-time high (Simpkins 2011). The EIA WTI crude price projections show that the $100/barrel price will most likely be reached this year, as indicated in Illustration 9 on the following page.

Therefore, given that the present price development is also

Illustration 9. WTI Crude Price Development in U.S. Dollars per Barrel

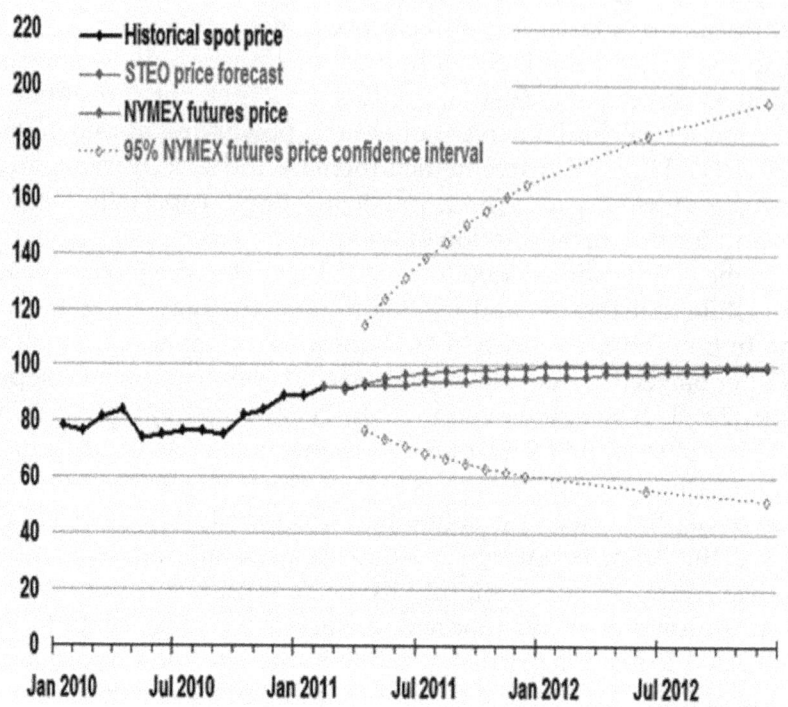

Source: EIA 2010c

above the reference case projections, as illustrated below, it seems highly likely that the future price development of crude, which is in the EIA study based on conventional drilling alone, will exceed the reference case projections, as shown in Illustration 10, p. 47.

The probability of rising crude oil prices and known increase in demand, especially from China and other rapidly growing nations, highlights both the huge potential profits to be made by the oil companies and also the urgent need to develop alternative fuels and implement new technologies to reduce CO_2 emission from all sources, especially from passenger cars. Faith Birol, Chief Economist for the EIA, notes in the organization's annual report that China's growing need for oil to meet domestic demand will have

Illustration 10. Historical Development and Projectionof World Crude Oil Prices

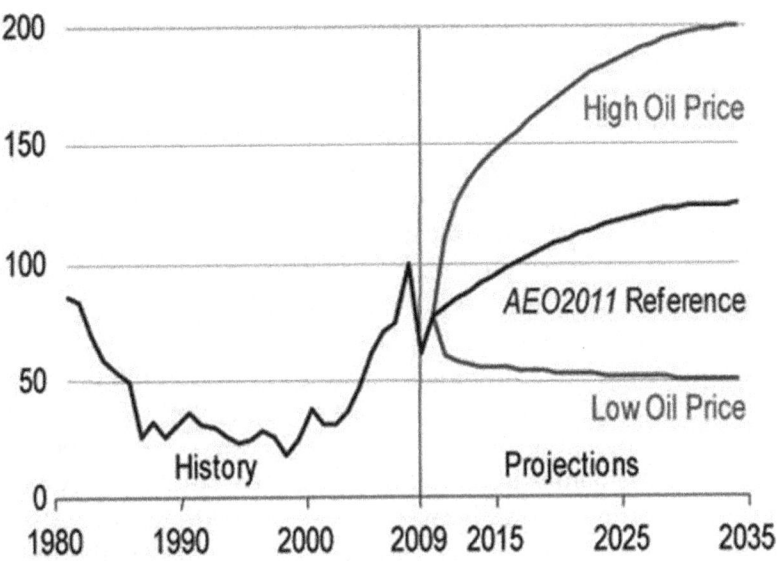

Annual average price of low sulfur crude oil
(real 2009 dollars per barrel)
Source: EIA 2010c

an increasingly large impact on international markets. She states, that in the U.S., 700 out of every 1,000 people own a car. In Europe, that rate is 500 out of 1,000. In China, the present rate is 30 out of 1,000. Birol predicts that rate could rise to 240 out of 1,000 by 2035 (EIA 2011c). If China successfulyl implements infrastructure measures requisite for transportation and the use of cars rapidly, the rate could be even higher, further pushing demand for oil, profits for the oil producing companies, and CO_2 emissions.

Gordon and Sperling provide an explanation of why, despite the known harmful effects of rising CO_2 emission levels, the oil companies are still so focused on petroleum production – profitability. They maintain, that after the Gulf Spill in April 2010, the oil companies have invested heavily in marketing campaigns, "designed to show that they are busy thinking up ways to supply tomorrow's cleaner energy" and that even though the oil companies do, indeed, invest more than the U.S. government and other industries spend on biofuel research, this is a "miniscule investment for the largest oil companies which each generate at least $150 billion per year in revenue and $10 billion or more in profit." As an example of the relation of expenditure in alternative fuel as compared to petroleum-related expansion expenses, Gordon and Sperling report that, "Exon-Mobile's multiyear algae investment [algae is also being investigated as a possible alternative fuel] amounts to one-half of 1 percent of its petroleum capital and exploration expenditures over the past five years" (Gordon and Sperling 2010, B3).

Another factor contributing to the oil industry's dampened enthusiasm for alternate fuel sources is the fact that, in the U.S. alone, it has sunk costs of capital investment in oil well, refineries, pipelines, and service stations of over $1 trillion. While Gordon and Sperling acknowledge that conventional oil supplies are peaking and the oil companies need to find alternative sources, they point out that "given the choice between oil – even oil that is ever dirtier and more dangerous to extract – and alternative fuels, the industry is still betting on the devil it knows. Big Oil is drilling deeper and finding ways to convert unconventional oil – petroleum extracted by means other than traditional wells, from sources such as oil sands, coal and oil shale – into gasoline, diesel and jet fuel." The U.S. Geological Survey has estimated that there is enough oil from unconventional sites to meet future rising demand. As Gordon and Sperling note, there is little incentive for the oil companies to change their successful business model and as oil prices approach the $100/barrel range, the cost of extracting oil from these unconventional sources will be more than offset by higher prices (Gordon and Sperling, 2010, B3).

The ramifications of this scenario characterized by continued drilling and refining of oil from ever dirtier and ever more dangerous sources has a threefold effect which, at best, is food for disturbing thought and, at worst, is alarming. As the extraction process becomes more dangerous in terms of safety and in terms of invasion into the earth's ecosystem, the probability of unpredictable repercussions in the form of negative impacts to the environment from human-induced activities, in addition to contributing to climbing CO_2 emissions, rises.

Second, as discussed previously, WTI crude is sweet and the ultimate choice for gasoline production. As the source of fuel becomes dirtier and more sour, the measures for the processing of the crude to reduce the sulfur content in order to make the crude suitable for the production of gasoline, will increase the cost of gasoline production which will be passed on to the customer twofold - at the pump and in the form of higher living costs due to increased costs of transportation for food, goods, and services.Third, and even more challenging will be the necessity of developing automotive engine technology which is cost effective and which may need to be designed to use dirtier petroleum with a higher sulfur content, thereby increasing the cost of automotive engine development and the risk of increasing automotive CO_2 emissions, should this not be able to be resolved with new technologies in the absence of readily available cost efficient alternate energy technologies for automobile engines.

The Government

The present situation in China, characterized by an increase in demand for automobiles, leading to increased gasoline consumption and rising CO_2 emissions, is reminiscent of the early development of the automotive industry in our own country, as previously discussed. The role of the government is also similar in two ways – with regard to the creation of an infrastructure to enable the growth of the passenger car industry and also the role of the government in the regulation of pollutants, specifically CO_2 emissions from passenger cars. These tasks, which in the past have been seemingly at odds, are converging as the possibilities of new technologies to curb automotive emissions arise. This discussion will provide an overview of the factors leading to the development of the infrastructure which enabled that motorization of the U.S. - the development of the interstate and urban highway systems. Second, the role of the government in regulating automotive emissions in the form of CO_2 via the Corporate Average Fuel Economy (CAFE) regulations will be investigated.

Historically, as shown in the previous discussion concerning the role of the oil industry and its relation to both the automobile producers and the government, there appears to be sufficient evidence to suggest that all three sector participants worked together to further the growth of the gasoline-powered internal combustion engine and establish a preliminary infrastructure for that growth, following the demise of the streetcar industry. Whether one believes the as of yet unresolved conspiracy theory, data show that the measures undertaken at that time did, indeed, lead to a significant increase in passenger car traffic, as the U.S. rapidly became the global motor car leader.

In *Mass Motorization + Mass Transit*, David Jones highlights several indicators of the growth of American motorization. He compares the per capita ridership of mass transit in the U.S. and Europe in 1909 and 1990. As can be seen below in Table 6, mass transit ridership in the U.S. declined over 50 percent during this period. With the exception of a significantly lesser decline in Paris, the two other leading world cities, London and Frankfurt, experienced a substantial, and in relation to the U.S. decline, over proportional increase in ridership of mass transit during the same period.

A comparison of the level of motorization of the G-7 nations from 1925 to 1950 shows an overall increase in vehicles per 1,000 population, with the U.S. leading the motorization of the world on this basis. (See Table 7, p. 51).

Table 6. Per Capita Ridership of Mass Transit in Selected Cities in 1909 and 1990

Cities	1909	1990	Decrease/Increase	as percent
New York	330	155	-175	-53.0%
Boston	280	114	-166	-59.3%
Chicago	295	96	-199	-67.5%
London	245	325	80	32.7%
Paris	345	295	-50	-14.5%
Frankfurt	200	436	236	118.0%

Source: Jones 2008

Table 7. Motorization Levels in the G-7 Nations in 1925 and 1950

	Vehicles per 1,000 pop. in 1925	Vehicles per 1,000 pop. in 1950
United States	172	314
Canada	75	186
Great Britain	20	70
France	18	59
Germany	4	22
Italy	3	16
Japan	<1	4

Source: Jones 2008

The rapid and expansive motorization of the U.S. was made possible by two main factors - economic strength and the coordinated effort of the government to implement an infrastructure to support this growth. In the 1920s, the U.S. was clearly the dominant global economic power, leading in all key economic indicators, while having a relatively low share of the world's population to support. As can be seen below in Table 8, the U.S. enjoyed the highest rate of motorization at this time and was also the world's leading producer and refiner of oil.

Table 8. U.S. Key Economic Indicators in the 1920s

Share of world population in 1927	6%
Share of world industrial output in 1928	39%
Share of world GDP in 1928	26 - 28%
Share of global motor vehicle production in 1927	85%
Share of global motor vehicle registration in 1925	81%
Share of world oil production in 1926	70%
Share of world oil-refining capacity in 1926	> 80%

Source: Jones 2008

Table 9. GDP and Motorization Trends in the G-7 Nations 1913-1950

	Increase in GDP per capita	Increase in vehicles per 1,000 pop.
United States	80.4%	314
Canada	67.2%	186
Great Britain	51.2%	70
France	40.4%	59
Germany	6.4%	22
Italy	36.5%	16
Japan	38.7%	4

Source: Jones 2008

Despite two world wars, the U.S. continued to be the leading global economic power and most highly motorized country in the world in 1950, growing faster than other G-7 nations, both in terms of Gross Domestic Product (GDP) and vehicle per population ratios from 1913 through 1950, as illustrated above in Table 9.

According to Jones, the responsibility for the development of the highway system infrastructure, which was required to support the motorization of the U.S., represented a gradual evolution. At the beginning of the twentieth century, cities possessed not only well-tended roads, but also the funds to maintain them, in contrast to rural areas which enjoyed neither of these advantages. The first federal funding for rural highways occurred in 1912, under the auspices of the U.S. Post Office, with the intent to reduce expenditures and improve efficiency of rural post delivery. In 1916, the Bureau of Public Roads, now the Federal Highway Administration, was created and placed under the responsibility of the Department of Agriculture. Federal funds continued to be invested in the expansion of rural road construction, with an emphasis on orderly investment and the professional engineering and administration of highways. This 1916 act required states to establish highway departments and, according to Jones, designate specific highway routes to be eligible for federal funding (Jones 2008, 69).

By 1941, the U.S. automobile market had become saturated. In 1921, total domestic sales were 1.55 million cars, of which 1.07 million were to new owners and 0.48 million represented replacement vehicles.New owners represented 68.8 percent of total domestic auto sales. By 1941, this relationship had changed substantially. In that year, of the 4.43 million automobiles sold domestically, only 52 percent were to new owners, the remainder representing replacement sales (St. Clair 1986, 125). St. Clair provides an explanation of the effects of saturation:

> The basic notion of saturation generally involved the ideas of chronic, institutional limitation on new demand.... To increase demand, in the context of a saturated automobile market, often required that new uses for the automobile be found. This then required that institutional or structural changes be made in the role played by the automobile in society (for example, multiple-car ownership, increased reliance on the automobile for transportation, and so on). Barring such changes, a chronic condition of demand limitation would persist. The automobile market would be saturated in relation to the existing structure of demand and the existing pattern of automobile use....Saturation is an interesting concept, because it was in efforts at overcoming it that many notable changes in the automobile industry were made. For example, annual model changes, the decline of price competition in the industry, planned obsolescence, "trading-up" strategies, and increasing barriers to entry were all the result, to one degree or another, of efforts at counteracting saturation (St. Clair 1996, 125-126).

Despite these strategic efforts on the part of the automobile producers to engineer a boost in demand, the market remained saturated. Alternatives to these industrial countermeasures were needed if the automobile market was to grow to allow for an increase in production as well as revenue and profit to the automobile producers. As previously discussed, the structural effect which was an impediment for the growth of the automobile industry was viewed by many as the streetcar (Rutledge 2006, 15). However, both the streetcar and the saturation of the automobile market were tied to the real structural impediment to growth of the automobile industry following the decline in the streetcar industry – the urbanization of the U.S. According to St. Clair, as of the 1930s, the automobile industry "sought to overcome saturation in the automobile market by seeking to remove the limitations that prevented an expansion of automobile use and ownership in urban areas". This would entail the restructuring of U.S. cities to be more conducive to automobile travel. According to St. Clair, this involved not only the elimination of the street car, as discussed above, but, more importantly, the creation of an urban-oriented Interstate Highway System (St. Clair 1996, 126).

Jones, like St. Clair, acknowledges the saturation of the automobile market and states that, "Clearly the increase in motorization that occurred from 1920 to 1930 was vastly greater that the increase that occurred from 1930 to 1940: 145 percent versus 11 percent" (Jones 2008, 91). Jones also acknowledges the interests of the automobile producers in increasing market growth through penetrating urban markets. However, departing from St. Clair's line of argumentation, Jones maintains that social, political, and economic forces were the true drivers of the growth of the interstate highway system and the impetus for governmental involvement. Homeownership played an important role.

In 1920, 41 percent of the U.S. non-farm population which lived in cities with a population greater than 4,000 owned a home. By 1930, this figure climbed to 46 percent. Before World War I, large scale housing development was negatively impacted by the limited availability of credit and low scale economies, as compared to single house construction. In 1914, the provision for a deduction for mortgage interest on income tax combined with rapid growth of installment credit and credit programs for automobiles after World War I, along with several other incentives at the local level, helped boost private ownership of homes in the nonfarm population by 12.5 percent between 1920 and 1930 (Jones 2008, 45).

In opposition to St. Clair, Jones argues that the U.S. was already on the trajectory toward mass motorization in the 1920s. Jones maintains that mass motorization in the U.S. would have occurred with or without either the New Deal or an aggressive program of metropolitan highway expressway construction. However, this would have taken place absent of uniform, active engagement of the states in urban freeway development or such thorough standardization of highway design and investment on a national basis (Jones 2008, 92). Jones concludes:

> In any event, it is crystal clear that the interstate and urban highway investment was legacies of the Depression and New Deal. It is also clear that the New Deal's commitment to a nationwide program of metropolitan highway development was financed with state and federal funds derived from fuel taxes and executed by highway departments with a statewide perspective and at least some insulation from urban politics was the only institutional framework that could have produced metropolitan freeway development of the ambition and ubiquity achieved by the interstate program. In turn, the long-term effects of urban expressways and the metropolitan beltways on household location options and urban development patterns – many beneficial, others not so beneficial – nominate the Great Depression and the New Deal, taken together, as another hinge event in the American history of motorization. (Jones 2008, 93)

Historically, the second major impact which the government has had on the growth of CO_2 emissions from passenger cars is the restriction of these through the imposition of limits which passenger vehicles are allowed to emit. These limits, Corporate Average Fuel Emission (CAFE) standards, were first introduced via the Energy Policy Conservation Act which was enacted to law by Congress in 1975. The act, which was passed in response to the Arab oil embargo in 1973-1974, and added Title V, "Improving Automotive Efficiency" to the Motor Vehicle Information and Cost Savings Act, established CAFE standards for passenger vehicles (cars and light trucks), with the goal of increasing new vehicle fuel economy by a two-told by the model year 1985 to 27.5 mpg. The executive responsibility for the establishment of CAFE standards is held by the Secretary of Transportation which delegated the authority to the Administrator of the National Highway Traffic Safety Administration (NHSTA). The NHSTA is responsible for all aspects of the regulation and administration of CAFE standards, including the classification of vehicles as passenger vehicles and "providing incentives such as credits for alternative fueled vehicle lines." The EPA is responsible for calculating the CAFE certification for each vehicle manufacturer (NHSTA 2011).

It is interesting to note that the initial CAFE target set in 1975 for the 1985 model year was 27.5 mpg. The NHSTA states that despite the fact that annual targets had been initially set from model year 1986 through model year 1989, the standards were lowered and thereafter, in 1990, the standard was amended to 27.5 mpg which was the original target for 1985. In 2006, the NHTSA released a final rulemaking for SUVs and light duty trucks which restructured the CAFE program to establish standards based upon vehicle size (Yacobucci and Bamberger 2007, i).

In March 2009, the U.S. Department of Transportation announced CAFE standards for 2011 model-year requiring cars to average 30.2 mpg and light trucks to average 24.1 mpg. The combined average fleet requirement was set at 27.3 miles per gallon, which is below the 1990 level of 27.5 mpg set for cars, and although this is a 2 mpg increase above the 2010 standard, represents only a 1 percent increase over the 27.0 mpg level for 2008 model year vehicles. The 27.3 mpg standard for model year 2011 cars is also less than the original target set in 1975 for 1985 model year cars at 27.5 mpg. The standard for cars, a 2011 average of 30.2 mpg, is 1.2 mpg less than the car fleet average already achieved for model year 2008 cars, according to U.S. Department of Transportation statistics (Hybridcars 2009).

On May 21, 2010, President Obama issued a memorandum entitled, "Improving Energy Security, American Competitiveness and Job Creation, and Environmental Protection Through a Transformation of our Nation's Fleet of Cars and Trucks". This memorandum announced that the NHTSA and the EPA would work on two joint rulemakings to improve fuel economy and reduce GHG emissions for the passenger vehicle sector and for commercial trucks, respectively. Standards were to be set for model years through 2016, with the goal of identifying potential standards which could be set nationally for the model years 2017-2025. This is the first time both agencies have been engaged in a joint rulemaking process for CAFE standards and is also the first time emissions control of commercial

Table 10. Federal Fleet Average CAFE Standards by Model Year 2012 – 2016 (mpg)

	2012	2013	2014	2015	2016
Cars	33.8	34.7	36.0	37.7	39.5
Light Trucks	25.7	26.4	27.3	28.5	29.8
Fleet	31.0	31.1	32.2	33.8	35.5

Source: Stein and Wernie 2011

trucks in the U.S. has been addressed. In addition, this is the first time that limits of GHG emissions from motor vehicles have been set. The NHTSA and the EPA sought input from the automobile producers and engine manufacturers, environmental organizations and various States, including California as well as the National Academies of Science (EPA 2010b). The target has been set at 35.5 mpg for 2016 model year light vehicles and a national average emissions target of 250 grams of CO_2 per mile driven, as shown above in Table 10 (Guilford b 2010, 24).

Even while this does represent an improvement, U.S. passenger vehicles that meet these standards will still, on the average, perform less efficiently in terms of miles per gallon than passenger cars in Europe and Japan (JATO Dynamics).

As mentioned at the beginning of this discussion regarding the government's role in the U.S. passenger car sector, the tasks of providing an infrastructure and supporting new alternative technologies which have, in the past have been seemingly at odds, are converging as the possibilities of new technologies to curb automotive emissions arise. The most evident example of this is the infrastructure to support the use of electric passenger cars. This involves two aspects of governmental influence - the power supply for electric vehicles, battery technology, and the infrastructure to charge these vehicles.

Battery technology for future viable electric vehicle programs in the U.S. is not well-established. The major source of environmentally friendly lithium-based batteries is the Asia Pacific region, with China and South Korea as the leading producers of non-lead acid batteries for electric vehicles. This represents a major cost impact for U.S. electric vehicles as the typical cost per cell averages about $100 and there are ten-fold multiples of cells necessary to power a passenger vehicle. As noted by Peter Whoriskey in *The Washington Post* on January 27, 2011, government incentives "are necessary to reach the goal [of 1 million electric vehicles on the road by 2015] because electric vehicles are so expensive, largely because of the cost of the batteries. The Chevrolet Volt is priced at $41,000 and the Nissan Leaf at $32,780, well above comparably sized cars with gasoline engines that can cost about $20,000" (Whoriskey 2011c, A12).

The second aspect regarding the successful launch of electric vehicles is the infrastructure requisite to support extended travel ranges. The typical, presently available electric vehicle has a range of approximately 100 miles and requires some eight hours to recharge (The Economist 2010b, 23). With the exception of some municipalities in California, mainly located around the Los Angeles area, there is neither nationwide nor any extensive citywide coverage of charging stations to support the use of electric vehicles. Substantial investment will be required to establish an infrastructure for charging across the nation. This will require a greater and more coordinated effort than that to establish the national highway system as the technology is not ripe and the solutions are not well-defined. This will also be the case for fuel cell-powered vehicles, which will require, for example, hydrogen filling stations along the nation's highways. The establishment of both the technology and the manufacturing in the U.S. as well as the creation of a nationwide system of easily accessible filing/charging stations for vehicles which operate on alternative fuels represent two of the greatest challenges facing and requiring the attention of the U.S. government today.

The Automobile Producers

Many of the relationships and influences of the U.S. automobile producers have already been discussed in the preceding sections regarding the oil industry and the government. This section will focus on the automobile producers' reactions to the government's push for increased fuel efficiency and the automobile producers' role in the development of new alternative vehicle propulsion technologies.

Table 11. 2010 Model Year CAFE Ratings and Comparison of 2010 Ratings with Future Standards – U.S. Passenger Cars

Model	Domestic	Import	2010 mpg	Future mpg standards
Toyota		x	44.4	
Honda		x	40.9	2015 37.7 mpg, 2016 39.5 mpg
Kia		x	36.6	
Toyota	x		36.4	2014 36.0 mpg
Nissan	x		34.8	
Honda	x		34.7	2013 34.7 mpg
Mazda		x	34.5	2012 33.8 mpg
Ford	x		32.3	
Mazda	x		31.4	
GM	x		30.6	
Chrysler	x		28.0	

Source: Stein and Wernie 2011

Recent data from the NHTSA shows that some automobile producers already meet the new CAFE standards for 2012 and some even met the 2016 limit today, i.e. Toyota and Honda imported cars. Ford, GM, Chrysler and Mazda domestically produced passenger cars do not meet the 2012 mpg requirement as of today, as shown above in Table 11.

The picture for the Big Three with regard to meeting future CAFE standards for light trucks is similar to that for their respective domestically produced passenger car ratings. The present efficiency ratings will not meet the new 2012 model year standards, as can be seen in the following Table 12, p. 59.

The main challenge for those automobile producers that do not meet the new standards with existing products is two-fold. The first is a challenge to the traditional CAFE strategies which the automobile producers have relied upon until now. This strategy was based on a pooled mix and provided the opportunity for the production of less fuel efficient and heavier light trucks and SUVs to be offset with more fuel efficient small cars. Under the new ruling, every producer will have its own CAFE requirement which will be sales-weighted by footprint, which is defined as the "area enclosed by

Table 12. 2010 Model Year CAFE Ratings and Comparison of 2010 Ratings with Future Standards - U.S. Light Trucks

Model	2010 mpg	Future mpg standards
Hyundai	30.0	
Subaru	29.9	2015 28.5 mpg, 2016 29.8 mpg
Mitsubishi	28.3	2014 27.3 mpg
Honda	26.9	
Mazda	26.6	2012 25.7 mpg, 2013 26.4 mpg
GM	25.4	
Chrysler	24.1	
Ford	24.0	

Source: Stein and Wernie 2011

the points at which the wheels meet the ground" (Guilford 2010c, 24). This means, that unlike in the past when automobile producers could "pump out stripped down econoboxes to balance out big, gas-guzzling trucks" and still meet the mpg ratings, "the more small cars they sell, the higher their CAFE number rises" (Guilford 2010b, 25).

The second and more daunting challenge is for those automobile producers that are far from meeting the new standards to find ways to re-engineer the vehicles so that they can pass the new standards. Three avenues are being pursued, which may help to jump start the introduction of new engine technologies and alternative propulsion sources for passenger cars in the U.S. - weight reduction, improvements to conventional engine and transmission technologies, and alternate propulsion systems of passenger vehicles. All of these developments will increase the cost of the vehicle which presents two major problems. First, the cost of these improvements will be passed on to the customer. The EPA has estimated that the new technology required to meet the 2016 standards will increase the sales prices of passenger vehicles by $1,300 per vehicle, on the average. However, most industry specialists believe the figure is extremely low. As reported by Stein and Wernie, Sandra Stokowski, President of See More Systems, a systems engineering group, has estimated that the cost of a compact car will increase by some $2,000 with prices for mid-sized vehicles rising $4,500 to $6,000. She estimated that the change over to a diesel engine from the typical V-8 gas powered engines in pickup trucks could, along with other necessary improvements, raise the sticker price of those vehicles up to $9,000 per vehicle (Stein and Wernie 2011, 24).

The true cost increase will be determined by the measures taken to reach the new standards. The cost increase creates a real and present dilemma for the automobile producers who have relied heavily on discounts and rebates in the past to maintain their sales volumes. There is widespread fear that rising sticker prices will lead to a downturn in demand, especially if the economic situation in the U.S. does not rebound quickly and to a level sufficient to offset the price increase. At the same time, the rising cost of oil will also lead to an increase in gas prices and higher overall prices due to rising transportation costs. In addition, the technology costs on compact cars will increase, which will diminish the incentive to downsize the U.S. vehicle fleet. Even such companies as American Honda Motor Co., which has been a traditional supporter of fuel economy regulations has expressed concern about increased costs negatively impacting demand and that the new standards may be more than the market can bear (Guilford 2011b, 25).

U.S. automobile producers are scrambling to meet the new standards. The most challenged are the Big Three's light trucks. As Stein and Wernie note, Rick Spina, who heads full-sized truck development at General Motors, recently reported that GM plans to reduce light truck vehicle weight by 500 pounds by 2016 and is investigating ways to reduce overall vehicle weight by some 1,000 pounds by 2020. Weight reduction requires costly materials such as aluminum and carbon fiber to replace sheet metal. It has been estimated that weight reduction through alternative materials costs about $2 per pound (Stein and Wernie 2011, 24).

In addition to weight reduction, engines and transmissions will also need to incorporate technology to improve fuel economy. Many of these technologies have been used in European and Japanese vehicles for several years. For example, continuous variable transmission has long been popular in Japan. Dual clutch transmissions which help to improve fuel economy are prevalent in European makes. Turbocharging, variable valve timing and variable lift systems, as well as cylinder deactivation to improve engine efficiency are options which could greatly improve the fuel efficiency and reduce CO_2 emissions for most models. Gasoline direct injection systems present a fuel efficiency option for compact to mid-sized cars and light trucks. The replacement of gasoline- powered engines with diesel engines and direct injection diesel engines can contribute to improved fuel economy as will a substantial increase in the employment of 4-cylinder engines, often two in one vehicle as a replacement for the less fuel efficient V-6 engines.

Hybrid vehicles, which alternate between using a gas powered engine and a battery as source of propulsion, depending on driving conditions, could help fill the strategic niche to meet CAFE standards. Electric vehicles are also being developed. However, the costs of procuring the batteries required for electric vehicles, based on present lithium technology are high and at present there is not an adequate infrastructure to support the growth of the electric vehicle. Alternate battery technologies are being investigated, but these will take years to develop.

Despite a lack of infrastructure for refueling of hydrogen powered vehicles, fuel cell technology, almost all major automobile producers are intending to enter into the market around the 2015 timeframe. These vehicles require neither gasoline nor electricity from an external source and also produce no emissions. According to Kranz in *Automotive News*, "The push for fuel cells is also fueled by the realization by automakers that the hybrid, the plug-in hybrid and battery-powered vehicles collectively will be unable to meet stiffer CO_2 regulations later this decade" (Kranz 2010a, 20H).

Selected examples of these technologies will be discussed in greater detail in the following Chapter as considerations for possible viable solutions to the problem at hand, namely, the need to significantly decrease CO_2 emissions from passenger vehicles in the U.S. to prevent further acceleration of climate change which is impacting our health and access to those resources necessary for human life. Before continuing to that discussion, this chapter will conclude the review of the participants in the U.S. passenger car sectors with a look at the consumer, who is becoming, increasingly, in the opinion of many automotive analysts, "the wild card" (Guilford 2010a, 24).

The Consumer

Unlike the times of the dawn of the motorization of America in the 1920s where the product offering was narrowly controlled by the automobile producers and demand was pushed by the oil industry and the government, today the consumer is at center of the demand cycle. The "wild card" effect is based on the fact that U.S. consumers are driving passenger car sales in a direction which is neither contributing to fuel efficiency nor decreasing CO_2 standards, despite real and well-supported data that this behavior is contributing to climate change and long-term devastating effects. As aforementioned, the cited Gallup Poll showed that, for the first time in twenty five years, U.S. Americans have ranked economic concerns higher than environmental concerns. This too, is confounding given that U.S. drivers are paying substantially more for heavier and inefficient vehicles than for smaller cars, which are more fuel efficient, pollute less, cost substantially less and are readily available.As of December 2010, sales of all passenger vehicles in the U.S. had increased 11.5 percent over the same period in 2009. The main increase was in the truck segment, specifically midsize SUV sales which increased 41.1 percent over the previous year, as depicted in Illustration 11 on the following page (p. 64).

As shown in Table 13, during this period, from 2009 to 2010, passenger car fuel efficiency in mpg increased on the average 2.4 percent for new models. The increase in fuel efficiency for light trucks, which were the main choice of U.S. passenger car consumers in that period, increased only half of that for passenger cars, 1.2 percent versus 2.4 percent. In addition, the relative performance in terms of mpg for light trucks, as compared to passenger cars, on the average, decreased by 1.6 percent . Relative to imported passenger cars, light trucks performed 3.6 percent less efficiently in 2010 than in 2009.

As reported by Whoriskey, sales of SUVs "jumped 41 percent during the first eleven months of the year [2010], led by vehicles such as the Jeep Grand Cherokee and the Honda Pilot, each which get

Illustration 11. Percentage Change in New Automobile Sales in the U.S. 2009 to 2010, Year to Date December 2010

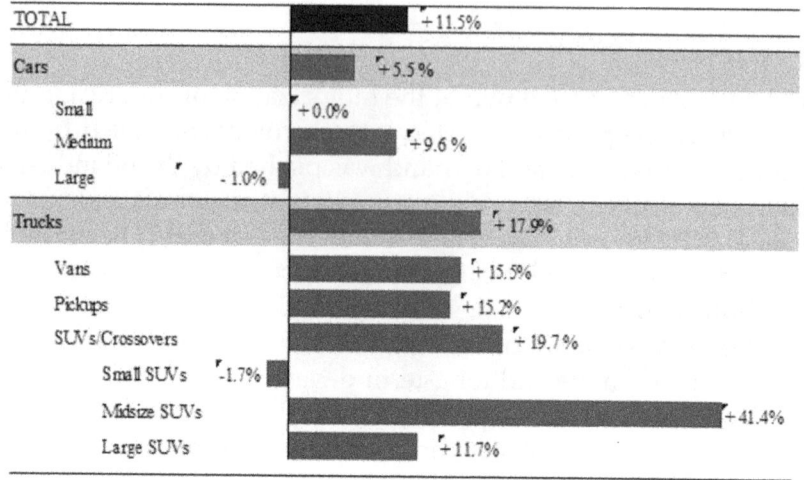

Source: Whoriskey 2010

Table 13. Average Fuel Efficiency of U.S. Passenger Cars and Light Trucks 2009 and 2010 in mpg

	2009	2010	Difference 2010/2009 as %
Passenger Car	32.9	33.7	2.4%
Domestic	32.1	32.9	2.4%
Imported	33.8	35.1	3.7%
Light Truck	24.8	25.1	1.2%
			Absolute Difference
Difference LT to Car	-32.7%	-34.3%	-1.6%
Difference LT to Import Car	-36.3%	-39.8%	-3.6%

Source: RITA 2010

about 18 miles per gallon. Sales of small cars, by contrast, remained flat despite otherwise surging demand for automobiles. Sales of the Toyota Corolla and the Honda Civic declined and even the fuel-sipping Toyota Prius, the hybrid darling of the eco-conscious, dropped 1.7 percent." He cites a quote from, Mr. Jackson, the chief executive of AutoNation, the largest automobile retailer in the U.S. Jackson maintains that, "You have about 5 percent of the market that is green and committed to fuel efficiency....But the other 95 percent will give up an extra 5 mpg in fuel economy for a better cup holder" (Whoriskey 2010, A1).

Jackson likens the consumer choice for small fuel efficient cars to the appeal of broccoli versus the popular American doughnut and notes that, "If you are selling both, most people are going to go for the doughnuts....As long as you have cheap fuel, it's hard to get people to buy what's good for them and good for the country....It's been the same for a decade" (Whoriskey 2010, A16).

A recent poll of automotive executives, including representatives from the Volkswagen Group of America, General Motors, BMW of North America, Daimler AG and Mazda North American Operations confirms Jackson's statement, "Automakers developing alternative power trains or small fuel-efficient cars face one crucial but wildly fluctuating variable: the price of gasoline" (Guilford 2011d, 22). As indicated in Table 14, gas prices have indeed fluctuated greatly over the period from September 2008, when the price of oil exceeded the $100/barrel mark and the price of gasoline hit an all time high of $4.11 per gallon and then three months later plummeted to a price below $2.00 per gallon. According to Guilford, during the period of the high price range, "automakers couldn't build fuel-efficient vehicles fast enough. But then prices plunged below $2 a gallon and public interest in fuel economy faded," as show in Table 14 p. 66 (Guilford 2011d, 22).

It could be assumed that the U.S. passenger vehicle consumer has become more price sensitive to fluctuations in gasoline prices due to increased commute or length of trip to drive to work. However, an analysis of vehicle and miles and trip lengths from 1969 to 2009 (Table 15, p. 66), shows that although the total number of miles driven per annum increased in that period by 38.7 percent, the number of annual miles driven to work increased only by 3.3 percent.

Table 14. U.S. Retail Gasoline Prices – Regular Grade September 2008 – January 2011 in US Dollars per Gallon

Date	Price per Gallon	Change from previous period in %
Sep-08	$4.11	
Jan-09	$1.60	-156.3%
May-09	$2.10	23.8%
Sep-09	$2.50	16.0%
Jan-10	$2.60	3.8%
May-10	$2.90	10.3%
Sep-10	$2.70	-7.4%
Jan-11	$3.10	12.9%

Source: Guilford 2011d

Table 15. Average Annual Vehicle Miles and Trip Length in the U.S. 1969 – 2009

Year	Travel to Work	Change 2009 vs. 1969	All trips	Change 2009 vs. 1969
Average annual vehicle-miles per household				
1969	4,183		12,423	
1995	6,492		20,895	
2001	5,724		21,171	
2009	4,325	3.3%	20,251	38.7%
Average annual vehicle trips per household				
1969	445		1,396	
1995	553		2,321	
2001	479		2,171	
2009	313	-42.2%	2,025	31.1%
Average vehicle trip length (miles)				
1969	9.4		8.9	
1995	11.8		9.1	
2001	12.2		9.9	
2009	13.9	32.4%	10.1	11.9%

Source: U.S. Department of Transportation 2009

Illustration 12. Sales of Passenger Vehicles and Gasoline Price Development in the U.S.

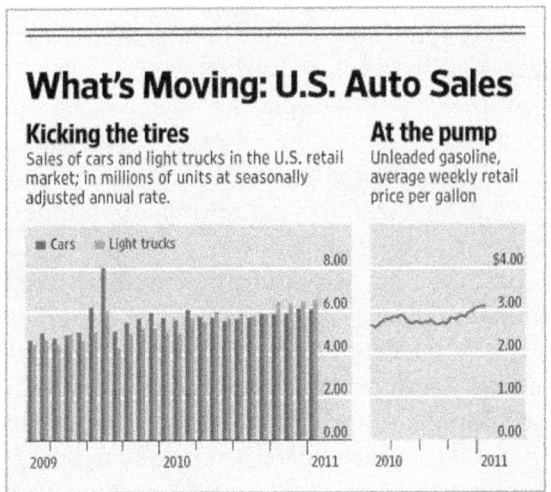

Source: Wall Street Journal Online 2011

On the average, Americans drive 13.9 miles to work and only 10.1 miles on other trips.

These data, regarding sensitivity to gasoline prices and driving behavior, appear to suggest that the consumer is the ultimate cost/benefit analyst in the U.S. Passenger Car System. However, a recent study presented in the Wall Street Journal Online, depicted above in Illustration 12, shows that despite rising fuel costs, Americans are buying more light trucks than cars, even though these larger vehicles are less fuel efficient, driving up not only the amount of emissions, but also the cost of operating the vehicle (Wall Street Journal Online 2011).

While markets prices appear to influence the economic behavior of the consumer, these latest data show that perhaps there are other aspects driving consumer behavior which needs to be considered. Two of these which will be briefly investigated are the psychological and physiological factors which influence American passenger car consumer behavior.

The role of the automobile in the psyche of American society is not to be underestimated. This discussion is not intended to be an in-depth sociological analysis of this topic, but rather a presentation of information which is intended to show that the American consumer has a unique relation to the automobile and to driving, and that this relationship which has historical roots and has developed over time, has been influenced by actions of the government, automobile producers and auxiliary industries, and does, indeed, impact the purchasing choices of American drivers.

James Womack et al in the book entitled, *The Machine That Changed the World*, baptized the automobile with that name (Womack et al 1990). According to Holden, "The powerful imagery of the car is like the car itself, ubiquitous. Inevitably such objects become metaphors and metonyms in which we choose part of reality to represent the whole. Its widespread use in film and literature as a metaphor for freedom, of 'moving on', and starting over is reflective of individualism and the need for control over one's destiny, concepts powerful in the West, especially in the USA" (Holden 1998, 29). Manning suggests that, "the automobile myth reached its apogee in the 1950s when the industry underwent an enormous boom, cars becoming fancier and faster ....The car became integral to American rituals" (Manning 1995, 33). Marsh and Collett maintain that the car became not only the symbol of the jet age, but also the symbol of American optimism as embodied in consumerism (Marsh and Collett 1986, 118). According to Holden, "Harold Macmillan's [the former British Prime Minister] election slogan, 'You've never had it so good' symbolized the new mass consumption era, which for Americans spelt out that anything is possible. Cars had become grounded spaceships to the frontier" (Holden 1998, 30).

Heining points out that cars have also been embedded in the music of the modern U.S., further underscoring the importance of the imagery of the car as freedom and, increasingly, a vehicle [no pun intended] of self-definition. He mentions that from Elvis Presley's pink Cadillac to John Lennon's white Rolls Royce and from Brian Wilson's *Little Dance Coupe* to Prince's *Little Red Corvette*, cars became the ultimate symbol of what it meant to be an American (Heining 1998, 96).

Seiler's work in *Republic of Drivers: A Cultural History of Automobility in America*, focuses on the importance of the automobile in a more deeply rooted sense than expressed by either Holden or

Heining. Seiler states that historian James Flink's assessment of the importance of the motor vehicle, the highway structure, and the emotional importance of the automobile for Americans is not just centered around cars and roads but, rather, is an array of concepts, institutions, objects, and practices which have been woven into the American society (Seiler 2008, 5). Seiler maintains that the automobility of the U.S. has, "established and delimited a horizon of agency, social relations, political formations, self-knowledge, and desire" (Seiler 2008, 6). Leed suggests that travel by automobile is a "demonstration of freedom and means to autonomy" (Leed 1991, 13). Seiler supports this notion and takes it a step further by maintaining that this freedom via automobile travel has established itself as a right in the U.S. He maintains that movement is linked to the ability to be productive and, ultimately, to capitalism, and that as a result, the person who is mobile is privileged to move unrestrainedly (Seiler 2008, 22-23).

Seiler states that in the 1920s, industry leveraged consumer anxiety regarding class, wealth, and gender through advertisement promoting solutions resulting from increased consumption by using the industry's ability "to meliorate politically significant polarities of wealth and access to goods, and to open to workers new avenues to the good life". He maintains that the figure featured in advertisement for goods and services of all types, including automobiles, "merged the individual of the marketplace with the ...autonomous individual", reassuring that the subjectivity determined by self-determination had survived.This new social self, he states, was characterized by mobility and choice, "and its embodiment was the driver". Seiler links this to the American perception of good citizenry, "Here consumption offered a direct link to republican citizenship, understood as a material stake in the stability of the current order" (Seiler 2008, 35). This aspect of the link between good citizenship and consumption established a basis for the promotion of the automobile in the ensuing years, especially in the 1950s and, according to Seiler and others, played a significant role in the public acceptance of the development of the National System of Interstate Highways.

The Highway System was approved as a public works priority in 1944, and had been "forcefully" promoted over the three prior decades by a group consisting of the oil, automotive, trucking, cement, rubber, insurance, chemical, and construction industries, financial institutions and media, as well as consumer and political groups and was known as "The Road Gang". Military leaders were also key players in the Road Gang. Seiler maintains that the military interest in the U.S. highway system stemmed from witnessing the German *Reichsautobahn* which aroused the desire to create an efficient network of highways in the U.S. to allow for the rapid movement of troops and material (Seiler 2008, 94). However, as Seiler notes, the *Reichsautobahn* was actually an anathema for the American fathers of the highway system, who realized that the "American doppelgänger would have to be justified within the ideological institutional structures" of America. To this end, he maintains that transportation analysts, especially those related to the automobile industry, claimed, "the distinguishing feature of American automobility to be its organic, democratic, grass roots evolution, emphasizing that it had achieved its dominance through incremental change and the public's increasingly enthusiastic stance toward an automobilized everyday life" (Seiler 2008, 95).

Seiler quotes Henry Ford II, who said the Americans had given automobility "an overwhelming public mandate" (Ford 1956). In 1956, the Ford Motor Co. published a pamphlet entitled *Freedom of the American Road*, in which the company emphasized that the American citizen, "has to stop thinking of his personal payment for highways, such as taxes, tolls, or property, as contributions to a vague someone else, and back the necessary measures as an investment of permanent value to his nation and himself" (Ford Motor Company 1956). Henry Ford II provided an explanation for the rationale of the title, by stating that, "This book is called *Freedom of the American Road* simply because we Americans have always liked plenty of elbowroom – freedom to come and go as we please in this big country of ours" (Ford 1956). George W. Romney, at the time CEO of American Motors and later the forty-third governor of the State of Michigan, before becoming Secretary of the Department of Housing and Urban Development, echoed Ford's message: "the modern highway was 'like the vehicles that created it...the product of the people, a thing made by the people for the people' " (Romney 1950, 221).

As reported by Seiler, a profile of President Eisenhower's federal highway administrator appointee, Bertram D. Tallamy, featured in *Life Magazine* in 1956, stated that, "though the interstate system is designed to relieve the worsening traffic jam, Tallamy predicts it will actually increase traffic by at least 50 percent" (Seiler 2008, 99). Seiler maintains that, "convincing citizens to spend more time behind the wheel was an endeavor most justifiably undertaken by the industries that increased driving would enrich: a series of 1950s advertising campaigns funded by the Ethyl Corporation [which, as previously mentioned grew out of a relationship with General Motors and Standard Oil], the American Petroleum Institute, and others encouraged drivers to 'Drive More…it gets cheaper by the mile!' and touted the low price of gasoline compared to other commodities" (Seiler 2008, 99).

Davies concurs with Seiler and addresses the concerted effort of the Road Gang to promote the motorization of the U.S. public through creating and leveraging the concept of the car as the ultimate realization of the American dream. In *The Age of Asphalt*, Davies offers a telling summary of the effects of this effort.

> In 1970, the zenith of the Age of Asphalt, Americans drove their automobiles more than one trillion miles and spent over $93 billion to buy, operate, insure, park, and build roads for their automobiles. Between 1955 and 1970, Americans had purchased nearly one hundred million automobiles.
>
> The automobile thus become a vital cog in the national economy. Out of a welter of small and highly competitive enterprises early in the century – Essex, Maxwell, Winton, Studebaker, Olds, LaSalle, Stutz, Chevrolet, Packard, Ford, etc. – there emerged by the 1920s a concentration of several large manufacturers. By the 1950s the "big three" of General Motors, Chrysler and Ford dominated the automobile markets. The automobile industry accounted for about one-sixth of the Gross National Product, if one includes manufacture, sales, repair, and such subsidiary "spin-off" industries as upholstery, insurance, glass, oil [oil as a lubricant not as fuel], rubber tires, and electronics. Whenever the nation's

economy turned "soft," to presidents from Truman through Nixon instinctively turned to devices to stimulate automobile manufacture sales. Thus in 1973, a total of 112,000,000 automobiles were registered in the United States: significantly, each had a life expectancy when new of just five years. And a well-conditioned American people readily accepted the fact of an annual automobile fatality number of over fifty thousand along with four million injured. (Davies 1975, 9)

Thus far, it has been shown that the U.S. automobile consumer is unique in his driving behavior relative to environmental and economic concerns. Despite the known negative impacts from the operation of gas powered engines contributing to increased CO^2 emissions and climate change, the of rising costs of ownership and economic hardship, we still, on the average, choose to drive larger, more expensive and less efficient vehicles. It has also been shown that this is partially due to an engraving on the American culture by industries and the government that driving is considered to be a fundamental right and an expression of our American freedom.

However, we are presently confronted with the dilemma that the object that was characterized and sold as securing our freedom has become our national enslavement. The U.S. is, compared to other nations, singularly reliant on individual transportation in the form of automobiles and trucks. The ownership of at least one, if not more than one vehicle per person has become embedded in our culture as a sign of realization of the American dream. If the automobile was intended to represent American freedom and has led to a dependency on this mode of transportation as a nation, we are very much on the path of entering into further dependency on larger, heavier, less efficient vehicles. We are rapidly becoming trapped in this even more environmentally unfavorable vehicle segment due to another U.S. phenomenon - our national problem of obesity. This point is brought into the discussion, not as a matter of health, which it certainly is, but as a pure pragmatic and practical argument. Many U.S. citizens cannot fit comfortably, if at all, into small, fuel efficient cars.

According to a report by the Associated Press, the Organiza-

Illustration 13. Estimated BMI Index for Males Over 15, 2010

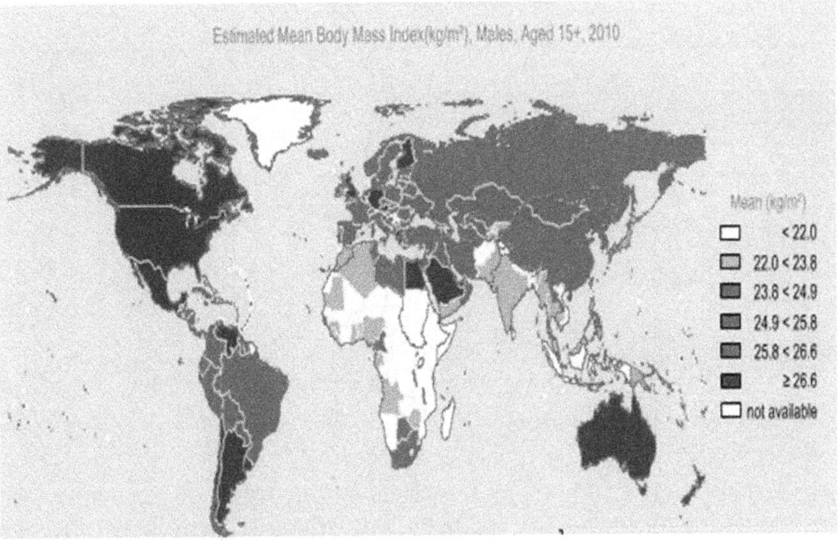

Source: WHO 2010

tion for Economic Co-operation and Development (OECD) stated in September 2010, in its first obesity forecast, that "citizens of the world's richest countries are getting fatter, and the US is leading the way". The OECD stated that in the US, the obesity rate was well under 50 percent in 1980 and has grown to some 70 percent in 2010. The organization estimates that 75 percent of Americans will be overweight or obese in 2020, "making it [the U.S.] the fattest country in the world" (Associated Press 2010).

The World Health Organization (WHO) defines obesity and overweight in terms of body mass index (BMI), measured by a person's weight (in kilograms) divided by the square of his or height (in meters). A person with a BMI of 25 is considered overweight. A BMI of 30 or greater is considered to be in the obese range (WHO 2011). The WHO data confirm the OECD data that the U.S. is the most obese country in the developed world, as can be seen above in Illustration 13 which shows the estimated global BMI distribution for males over the age of 15.

The U.S. Center for Disease Control reports that the average U.S. male over twenty years of age weighs 194.7 pounds and has

Table 16. Pricing, Mileage, Interior Room Selected 2011 Model Year Ford Passenger Cars

	Fiesta	Expedition (large SUV)	F150 Pick up
Base model cost	$13,320	$37,070	$22,415
mpg (city/hwy)	29/40	14/20	17/23
Front Shoulder Room	52.7"	63.2"	66.6"
Front Hip Room	50.6"	60.2"	60.5"

Source: Ford Motor Company 2011

a waist measurement of 39.7 inches. For women of the same age group, the average weight is 164.7 pounds and girth is 37.0 inches (Center for Disease Control 2009). As a basis for comparison, a report by the U.K. Department for Trade and Industry which detailed 294 measurements of Europeans, states that the Britons' average weight and girth is the largest in continental Europe, but still well below that of Americans. The study reports that the average weight for men was 175.8 pounds. The average female weight was 147.0 pounds with a corresponding average girth of 33 inches (Carvel 2002). This indicates that on the average, American men weigh almost 10 percent more than their British counterparts, who are reported to be the heaviest Europeans. American women, on the average, weigh almost 11 percent more than their British counterparts and have waists which are 12 percent wider.

As shown above in Table 16, comparison of the shoulder and hip room dimensions for the front seats of three U.S. Ford models shows that the most popular vehicle in the U.S., the F150 pickup, offers an additional ten plus inches versus the small car Fiesta.

While the increasing girth and weight of Americans and the relative increase in seat space may not be the sole factor to explain why the F150 has been the best selling model of all U.S. passenger vehicles since 2000 (Lasse 2010) and into the first months of 2011 (Automotive News 2011), this may well be a contributing factor to the vehicle's popularity, despite the price and poor fuel economy ratings. In the years 2000 through 2009, the F150 was rated at an unchanged 14/29 mpg city/highway (Lasse 2010). The rating for the latest 2011 model is 17/23 mpg city/highway. Although the fuel efficiency for city driving has improved, the highway rating has deteriorated over past model years.

This chapter has provided an overview of the participants in the U.S. passenger car sector and their relations over time. The oil industry has played a key role, in cooperation with the automobile producers and, at times, with the support of the government at the municipal, state, and federal levels to promote the growth in the number of passenger vehicles driven, specifically those with gasoline powered internal combustion engines.It has also been shown that despite the fact that alternate vehicle technologies have been available for over a century, these have not been actively developed by the automobile manufacturers who have relied almost exclusively on gas powered internal combustion engine technology for the propulsion of passenger vehicles.

It has also been shown, that certain automobile producers and members of the oil industry have worked with the government to create an infrastructure which promoted the expansion of passenger car utilization via the construction of the Interstate Highway System and the necessary auxiliary infrastructures, such as gasoline stations and streets in the urban centers of the U.S. The role of the government has been shown to be supportive of the expansion of automobile utilization not only through the creation of the Interstate Highway System, but also through the easing of policy measures which could have negatively impacted the growth of certain market segments in the passenger car industry. These measures include the issuance of stricter fuel economy standards which would lead to a reduction of CO_2 emissions as well as the regulation of fuels which contained lead in and were first banned in 1996, despite public knowledge of the negative effects of lead on human health. The government has been slow to allow the use of blended gasoline such as ethanol blends which have been proven to reduce emissions without negatively impacting engine performance.

The possibilities which Americans enjoy in terms of availability of relatively inexpensive gasoline, a broad range of available passenger car models, and the extensive system of urban streets and the national highways, which have been made available due to the collective efforts mentioned above, have led to the result that most Americans feel that the ownership and use of a passenger vehicle is a right, rather than a privilege. It has been shown that the car has become a part of the American psyche, imbued in our sense of freedom characterized by the right to travel unrestrictedly and as an expression of what it is to be an American - free, a good citizen, and contributing to the national good.

However, as discussed in the final section of this chapter concerning the consumer, what was intended to be our freedom has actually in many ways enslaved us as our dependency on the passenger car as a mode of transportation has become almost a necessity. The consumer is increasingly the wild card in the game, as the influence of the other three sector participants has diminished over time. At the beginning of the twentieth century, the automobile producers and the oil industry defined the rules of how the system operated. In the ensuing post-war period they were joined by the government to further the proliferation of passenger cars via the construction of the Interstate Highway System.

The convergence of these movements - the continued focus on the gasoline powered internal combustion engine and the expansion of our national roadways created the situation of lock-in and path dependency which we are in today. Kline defines lock-in as a result of positive feedback regarding a product which is so self-reinforcing that it leads to continued proliferation of a product which is technologically inferior because it is the leading choice of the consumer (Klein 2001, 97). Once a product is locked-in, that industry tends to move to the situation of path dependency due to consumer acceptance, but more importantly, due to the substantial cash invested for the development of the product and often enormous capital investments in equipment to produce that technology (Durlauf 1998, 160). The most commonly used example of path dependency is the QWERTY keyboard which was the basis for the placement of keys on the typewriter and is now found on almost all computer keyboards and electronic communication devices, such as cell phones. While though the QWERTY keyboard layout makes no logical sense and must be learned in addition to the alphabet, the fact that so many companies are so heavily invested in the production of products using the QWERTY system, render the costs to retool and redesign products which would use a more logical system, such as the alphabetical order, prohibitive.

The oil industry, the automobile producers, and the government have collectively contributed to the creation of a situation where the U.S. is path dependent on the gasoline- powered passenger car. In addition, the consumer has contributed to the problem in two ways. First, as has been shown, Americans tend to purchase larger, less efficient vehicles regardless of gasoline prices or economic impact in terms of purchase prices. The second and growing impact of the U.S. passenger car consumer contributing to a path dependent effect is indirect and could almost be overlooked. This effect, as has been discussed, is the growing obesity of the U.S. population which may well lead to the situation where the majority of Americans cannot fit comfortably into a small, fuel efficient vehicle.

If the argument holds, that we are path dependent on the use of large gasoline-powered vehicles, despite the fact, as has been discussed, that these vehicles are the single most largest contributors to atmospheric CO_2 emissions in the U.S., which have been shown to have exceeded a level considered unsafe for human health and are rapidly rising, the situation seems dismal. And as the sector participants increasingly operate as independent actors, and not with the concerted effort which contributed to the growth of the passenger car industry in the past, when the oil industry and automobile manufacturers with the support of the government represented a central authority promoting the car as in, the situation seems very diffuse and unpredictable. The erosion of the central authority is also due, in part, to the fact that the U.S. is no longer the sole supplier of domestic oil but is dependent on foreign sources of oil which determine, ultimately, the price of transportation in this country.

This analysis has also illustrated that the only common motivational force shared by all sector participants is the economic factor in the form of the relation of cost to benefit. However, the assessment of costs and accrual of benefits is becoming more difficult, especially as the U.S. economy is increasingly impacted by global events outside of its control, as evidenced by the most recent events in the Middle East and the corresponding effect on rising oil prices. There is both peril and promise in this situation, the discussion of which will continue in the following fourth and final chapter.

IV.

Peril or Promise: Future Possibilities for the U.S. Passenger Car Industry

It has been established that we, as human beings, share a binding intergenerational responsibility to ensure that all human beings, including those of future generations have access to those resources necessary to support human life. It has been shown that we have, with certainty, created the possibility that present and future generations may not have access to these resources due to the effects of climate change resulting from human activity, specifically, that the effect of increasing CO_2 emissions from gasoline-powered passenger cars in the U.S.

In Chapter III, it was shown that all participants in the U.S. passenger car sector have, over the course of the past one hundred plus years, individually and collectively, promoted the use of gasoline-powered vehicles. We are at a point where we are locked-in to this technology as the primary and almost sole means of ground passenger transportation in the U.S. and have reached a state of path dependency on the gasoline-powered passenger car.

It has also been shown that the motivational and situational forces driving the behavior of the sector participants have, in the past, been mainly commensurate and that these have, over time, become increasingly incommensurate with perhaps only a single common denominator, the economic factor. However, even given the common economic motivation, the costs and benefits for the sector participants are becoming more divergent. The situation seems almost insurmountable with no possibility of a solution. It appears that we are headed on a one way path to peril and further endangerment of the human race.

This chapter will build upon the information presented in the previous chapters to propose that, while we are a point in time which appears to be a doomsday scenario, there is also promise in the situation. I will frame the discussion of such promise by a very brief investigation of the postmodern era in which we find ourselves. Postmodernism is typically the subject of philosophical discussion. It is relevant to this thesis because it provides a deeper understanding of the situation within the passenger car sector in yet another historical context, that of our society's place in time.

Thereafter, I will propose concrete actions which could lead away from the path dependency we are now on and result in the short term realization of solutions to combat CO_2 emissions from passenger cars in the U.S. These will consist of proposals with regard to certain U.S. policies and also with regard to selected automotive engine technologies. These proposals, while appearing to be straightforward, are neither simple, nor will they be openly embraced by society at large and by all of the sector participants. But at the least, they highlight a realistic and achievable solution to the pollution problem and can help toward reducing CO_2 emissions from passenger vehicles in the U.S., thereby taking a major step towards ensuring that all human beings, regardless of their place in time have access to breathable air.

The term postmodern describes the period which began at the end of the nineteenth century, concurrent with the rise of industrialism and the beginning of the development of motor vehicles, and continues into the twenty first century. "These some one hundred and fifty years are the immediate history and context in which we find ourselves today and any claims regarding truth or what actions we need to take have to be made out of this historical context" (Ambrosio 2009). During this period, the automobile was developed and established as the main mode of passenger transportation in the U.S. As has been shown in Chapter III, the U.S. passenger car sector has undergone a transformation from a relative central authority exercised by the automobile manufacturers and oil industry at the beginning of the twentieth century shifting to the government and the automobile manufacturers in the 1950s. Presently, as has been discussed, the central authority in the sector has been greatly diminished and has become diffuse.

The historical relevance, as discussed in Chapter III, regarding the American psyche, is that we have come to view the automobile as the technological embodiment of our freedom, that quality of life sacred to the American dream. Sim maintains, that over time, the belief that quality of life could be improved without end and that science and technology would guarantee this has been called into question. "Postmodernity…is the state where skepticism is expressed about notions like the inevitable march of progress, or the necessity to continue exploiting the environment around us, irrespective of the long-term effect" (Sim 2009, 290). Furthermore, and also in line with what has been discussed in this thesis, postmodernism is characterized by the recognition of the coexistence and tension between two incommensurate forces which motivate human behavior and influence decisions – personalism/community versus impersonal individuality.

The discussions in both Chapters II and III highlighted how all sector participants have made and are, with time, increasingly making decisions which favor the individual rather than the community with the knowledge that, as a consequence of those decisions and actions, they are committing to increased risk of further environmental degradation due to CO_2 emissions from passenger cars in the U.S., leading to increased risk to the human community of today and tomorrow. In *Postmodernism and the Environmental Crisis*, Gare maintains that the environmental crisis is the most significant factor of the development of postmodern thought, because it reveals that what have tried to accomplish, in the name of progress, is for naught and that it is the "ultimate source of disorientation" (Gare 199, 5-6). He quotes Richard Newbold Adams:

> The nineteenth-century vision of how to make ideology for a vast colonial expansion and it was the world a better place in which to live was called 'progress.' It was a coal-fueled ideology for a vast expansion….Development is the successor to the vision of progress that accomplished the petroleum-fueled spread of industrialism in post World War II nationalizing. If the illusion of progress was dashed

by the First World War, the 'development' illusion began to crack and fragment, on the one hand, with increasing poverty, social movements and revolts, military interventions and regional wars, and, on the other hand, environmental pollution and degradation. (Adams 1998, 234)

In addition, postmodern philosophy provides a foundation for the chance of optimism in this discussion of our present situation regarding climate change resulting from CO_2 emissions from passenger cars. It appears that there is no solution. However, the recognition and acceptance of the possibility of the coexistence of incommensurate ideas, a feature of postmodern thought, opens the door for discussion and dissention. As Lyotard maintains, "... invention is always born of dissension. Postmodern knowledge is not simply a tool of the authorities, it refines our sensitivity to differences and reinforces our ability to tolerate the incommensurable"(Lyotard 1984, xxv). Lyotard echoes the sentiment of many of his contemporary philosophers who discuss the relevance and the application of postmodern philosophical thought to scientific undertakings. This process is characterized by groups of experts who may well have diverging and incommensurate ideas and goals, engaging each other by entering into a dialog in which all of the participants agree on a common set of rules and language, with the understanding that the goal of the dialog is consensus (Lyotard 1984, 65-66).

Bill McKibben, a well known environmentalist, also supports this postmodern view of communal problem resolution, albeit indirectly. In his latest book, *Eaarth: Making a Life on a New Tough Planet*, McKibben maintains that we humans have so changed the world through our activity, which has led to massive environmental degradation, that our planet is now no longer the earth of the past. He dubs this changed planet Eaarth He states, "We no longer live on the flat earth that Thomas Friedman postulated. Eaarth is an uphill place now...with more friction that we're used to" (McKibben 2010, 86). "There's too much friction, we're on an uphill planet, so we'd better change" (McKibben 2010, 97). He maintains, "The momentum of the heating [global warming due to climate change] and the momentum of the economies that power it, can't be turned off quickly enough to prevent hideous damage. But we will keep fighting in the hope that we can limit that damage. And in the process with many others fighting similar battles, we'll help build the architecture for the world that comes next, the dispersed and localized societies that can survive the damage we can no longer prevent. Eaarth represents the deepest of human failures. But we must still live on the world we've created – lightly, carefully, gracefully" (McKibben 2010, 211).

In line with postmodern thinking and personalism, McKibben suggests that dialog will provide the solution. In referring to his concept of the "uptick of neighboring", McKibben quotes Keith Hampton of the University of Pennsylvania, "I don't think people will create silos and hide in houses to shield themselves from hard times. They're going to look for people to help solve those problems. These tend to be your neighbors" (Hampton 2009).

Mike Tidwell, founder and director of the Chesapeake Climate Action Network and noted author and filmmaker takes the opposite, impersonal view. In his recent article entitled, "Weather Beaten" in *The Washington Post*, Tidwell describes how he has fashioned his home into a solitary fortress complete with locks, a generator, and a garden in the basement, capable of withstanding the effects of climate change and the insurgencies which he predicts will take place in this country due to resource shortages caused by climate change. Tidwell resides in Takoma Park, Maryland. There is no talk of neighborly uptick. He maintains that climate change is a real, present, and increasing danger and that we need to protect our individual selves. "Ten years ago I put solar panels on my roof as an act of love for the planet. Now I'm making new changes, focused on my immediate loved ones. The era of consequences, at every conceivable level, has entered our world. Ready or not" (Tidwell 2011, B1, B5).

These two points of view represent, in my mind, the peril. On the one hand is the peril, á la Tidwell, that we will either withdraw into our own cocoons of safety and individual protection to the extent that we continue on with our own lives without contributing to the communal effort to try and address the problem we have created. On the other hand, the peril also lies in complete reliance on dialog and consensus, which I maintain will not be possible in the short term. Driven by short term economic benefits which accrue to each of the sector participants at the cost of another and in a sector where, although, each of the participants speaks a common language, English, the terms and meanings used to communicate in each sector have specific meanings, consensus will be difficult, if not impossible, to reach. The peril in this increasingly self-organizing system of the U.S. passenger car sector is that either an ineffective solution, born of compromise, is identified and implemented, or that nothing is undertaken and the status quo remains unchanged.

The promise, conversely, is the fulfillment of the Kantian *sui generis* duty to ensure that measures are defined and enacted, to make the right and hard choices which need to be made, thereby creating positive collective action to reduce CO_2 emissions from passenger vehicles in the U.S. I propose that in the short term, a strong stance representing a central authority will be required to define and manage a program to combat the problem of environmental degradation due to CO_2 emissions from passenger cars in the U.S. This can be complemented with the approach which encourages dialog and consensus, but must, due to the urgency of the situation and the need to act, takes immediate precedence.

As expressed in words of former President Kennedy, in crisis, there is promise: "In the Chinese language, the word 'crisis' is composed of two characters, one representing danger and the other, opportunity." (Kennedy 1960). Taking on this task, which will be detailed below is not a campaign to become everyman's darling, but will require an in depth knowledge of the issues, conviction that truly have an opportunity and that we can implement positive changes, accompanied by the will to dare to do something different, difficult, and most likely unpopular and controversial.

I maintain that this effort must be led centrally by the Federal Government. I do not mean that one of the various existing agencies should be given authority for what I am proposing. The past has shown how convoluted and ineffective the workings of the majority of these agencies have proven to be. Rather, I specifically propose a select, small task force composed of industry experts which reports directly to the President. This method which proved to be successful in moving difficult issues forward in times of urgency where specific and expedient action was required, such as in the case of the financial bail out in the past two years. This group's purpose is not to find absolute consensus but, rather, to define and implement measures which require immediate attention and affect all participants in the U.S. passenger car sector. It has been shown that the goals and economic striving of the participants are so divergent that consensus is, at best, difficult, in reality improbable, as the U.S. passenger car system becomes increasingly complex and unpredictable and is increasingly characterized by incommensurate ideas such as the cost to make cars environmental friendly versus cost to consumer who is unwilling to pay.

Perhaps, more importantly, the recommendation to have this group report to the central authority of the President is due to the economic considerations which drive the decisions of the participant groups in very different directions and also are a reflection of the financial situation of the country. Unlike in the days of the birth of the automobile industry and during the times of the rollout of the National Highway Interstate System, in which the U.S. dominated the globe in terms of production and economic power as well as oil production, the country is now suffering deeply. According to a recent report, U.S. debt has risen to post World War II levels. At that time, federal debt, including the debt purchased from the Social Security Trust Fund, was approximately 122 percent of national GDP. The states and municipalities were virtually debt-free. Federal debt declined rapidly thereafter and, in the 1950s, was about 75 percent of GDP. The rapid decline can be attributed to a rapid economic growth fueled by increased productivity delivered by a young work force (Mufson 2011b, A10).

Today, the work force is aging. The U.S. lags behind Europe and Asia in terms of productivity. And, not only has federal debt climbed to staggering levels, but, unlike in previous times, states, municipalities, and consumers are also heavily indebted, if not bankrupt. Although gross federal, state, and local debt as a percentage of GDP is at 94.3 percent, lower than in 1946, on a percentage basis, it has risen to a level of $13.8 trillion in 2010, whereby combined state and local debt is $2.4 trillion. The 2012 fiscal budget proposed by President Obama indicates that "the federal government's net interest payments (not including money owed the Social Security Fund) will rise from 1.4 to 3.4 percent of GDP over the next decade" (Mufson 2011b, A10).

Given the dire economic situation, the focus of all of the participants in the U.S. passenger car sector on individual cost-benefit results, and the immediate need to act decisively to identify and implement known and proven measures to combat rising CO_2 emissions, I therefore recommend that the group report directly to the President. We are in the same situation as at the time, some two years ago, when the financial bubble burst - we have no time to remain complacent. And like, the time of the bubble burst, we are also dealing with a self-made problem resulting in an issue which affects not only our lives, but if not addressed, will burden the lives of future Americans.

As a prelude to the ensuing discussion it is important to reiterate two points. The first is that we are, at best, running out of time. The hour glass has tipped, as we have already crossed the 350 ppm CO_2 level which is dangerous for human health and, as been discussed in Chapter II, we are racing toward a level of 650 ppm. We simply have no time to waste by investing in endless, convoluted discussions and projects of unknown dimensions, however noble their lofty goals might sound. We need to act immediately and decisively. There are known solutions. We have no time to accommodate everyone and everything and create an aura of warm comfort. We are, as has been shown, on the brink of impending disaster in the form of change to our present way of living, threatening not only our existence but endangering the future of the human race.

The second point is that we cannot afford to invest in programs, endeavors, and projects which divert our attention and resources, both in term of manpower, intellectual force, and financial resources from the goal of doing our best to combat rising CO_2 emissions from passenger cars. While alternate modes of transportation and some new concepts of automobile propulsion, which represent the attempt of recreating the feeling of the freedom of endless travel are emotionally appealing and are the stuff of engineers' dreams, we have insufficient resources to pursue any path other than that which has already been blazed, and which requires some fine tuning of our direction, but does not entail significant redirection or reengineering. Our days of "go west young man" are over. Our wagons are stuck in a self-created quicksand of technology and economics, and we need to get out of the self made rut in a most expedient manner– for ourselves and those to come after us.

The program I recommend would consist of the initiatives which will be presented in the following portion of this section of the chapter as depicted in Illustration 14 on the next page.

These proposals are grouped into short-term and mid-term initiatives. The short- term initiatives include four policy related measures and the implementation of a new program, the U.S. Clean Car Program. The mid-term initiatives include two programs which are fundamental to the U.S. issue of emissions from passenger cars, but also have international dimensions. However, I submit that these two initiatives be resolved on a national level before attempting to enter into international discussion. The ease of implementation indicator is my personal evaluation of this measure. I do not suggest that the implementation of any of these measures will be easy. However, as the sphere of involvement in the definition and management of these initiatives moves from the government to the automobile suppliers and the consumer, increasingly by definition, the number of participants and the impact to these groups grow accordingly, and implementation will require more focused negotiation. This is what I define as the measure of the ease of implementation.

Revised Transportation Policy for the U.S.

I propose two policy changes and two tactical changes. The two policy changes are the initiatives Postponement of the High Speed Interstate Rail System and Change to Electric Vehicle Policy. The two tactical proposals are an Increase in Federal Fuel Tax on Gasoline and Reinforcement of CAFE Standards. The present Obama Administration has proposed two major plans which will impact the development of transportation in the U.S., namely the Federal Railroad Administration's plan for high speed intercity passenger rail systems and the most recent 2012 fiscal budget for electric vehicles. I argue that both of these measures should not be undertaken at this time and will provide explanations to support this view. The third policy related issue is with regard to the present management of taxation of fuel for vehicle use in the U.S. I propose a revision to the government's position on fuel taxation which includes a standardization of taxation at the federal level, in the form of an in-

Illustration 14. Proposed Initiatives to Reduce CO_2 Emissions from the U.S. Passenger Car Sector

Timing of Implementation	Initiative Title	Ease of Implementation
Short Term (1-2 years)	Revised Transportation Policy for the U.S. o Postponement of High Speed Interstate Rail System Proposal o Change Electric Vehicle Policy o Implementation of Revised Fuel Taxation o Reinforcement of CAFE Standards	
Mid-Term (2-3 Years)	U.S. Clean Car Program	
	Creation and Implementation of Sharing of Technology for the Environment Program (STEP)	
	Establishment and Completion of Project to Define Environmental Economic Metrics for the U.S.	

creased tax on gasoline, but not on diesel fuel. Fourth, I will make a proposal with regard to CAFE standards for those vehicles which do not and have no chance of meeting the 2012 model year standards (Note: The 2012 model year begins in the early fall of 2011).

On April 16, 2009, President Obama announced his vision for a new U.S. high-speed intercity rail system, "Imagine whisking through towns at speeds of over 100 miles an hour, walking only a few steps to public transportation, and ending up just blocks from your destination. Imagine what a great project that would be to rebuild America." The announcement further notes that the Interstate Highway System took over fifty years to complete, so that the true potential of an integrated high speed intercity rail system could not be realized overnight. In a statement which sounds very similar to those made regarding the introduction of the Interstate Highway System, as discussed in Chapter III, the Department of Transportation announced that, "Implementing these ...projects and programs will serve as a catalyst to promote economic expansion (including new manufacturing jobs), create new choices for

Illustration 15. Map of Proposed High Speed Interstate Rail System (Source: The Economist 2010c)

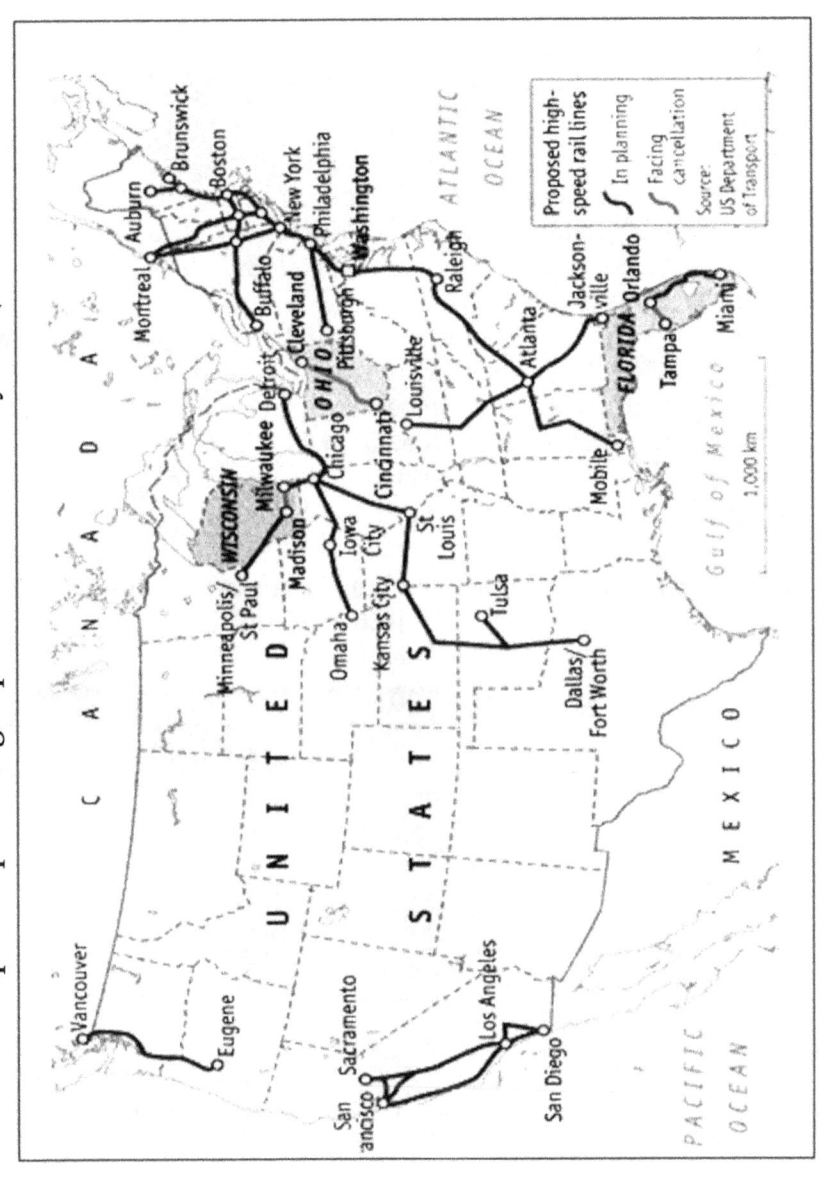

Source: The Economist 2010c

travelers in addition to flying or driving, reduce national dependence on oil, and foster livable urban and rural communities". The sum of $8 billion has been allocated for this project (Federal Railroad Administration 2009).

However, whisking across the country is a reality which is far from being certain or available, or even attractive. Presently, a one-way train trip from Washington D.C. to Los Angeles on March 22, 2011 with Amtrak costs $310 and entails approximately 36 hours of travel time (Amtrak 2011). A one-way plane trip on the same day from Washington D.C. to Los Angeles, in comparison, can be purchased for $149 and the travel time is slightly more than 6 hours (Orbitz 2011).

And, as shown in Illustration 15 (p. 89), the proposed Interstate High Speed Rail System is a far cry from a national system and is, in fact, a regional system. As can be seen, three of the proposed lines are facing cancellation in Florida, Ohio, and Wisconsin

I suggest that this rail project, at the present time, is not worth the investment and distraction, given the urgent need to address

Illustration 16. HSR Construction Costs per Mile for Selected Global HSR Projects (in $ million)

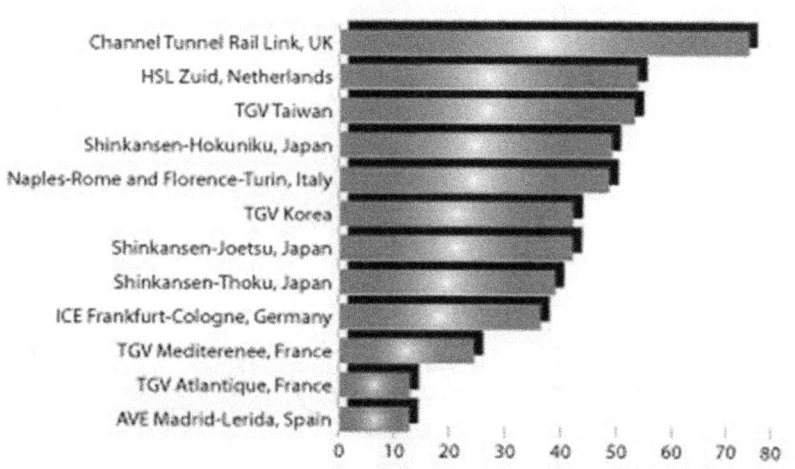

Source: SBI Energy 2010

and mitigate the passenger car emission problem. I maintain, along with the other measures described below, that the U.S. focus should be on improving fuel efficiency of automobiles rather than investing in a new rail system at this time for four reasons. First, is that we have an available and functional infrastructure for passenger cars and do not need to invest in new infrastructures. Second, is the issue of availability and familiarity with the technology to be invested in and to be implemented. We have the technology to improve the efficiency of passenger cars, as will be discussed. High speed rail technology is new for the U.S. Japan's Shinkansen bullet train system and the German Inter City Express (ICE) have both required substantial investment, years of development, and have been refined over time as the requisite infrastructure that was already in place has been further developed.

A recent study by SBI Energy compares the technologies of various high speed rail systems (HSR) and the costs associated with these systems, including the major systems which are presently in operation, shown in Illustration 16 (p. 90). A comparison of the construction costs per mile in millions of dollars shows that high speed rail systems which are in operation have ranged from some $12 million dollars per mile for the AVE Madrid-Lerida system high speed rail system in Spain to over $80 million per mile for the Channel Tunnel Rail Link in the UK, whereby it must be noted that when considering the high cost per mile of construction for the latter system it must be kept in mind that this high speed rail system is the system which runs in the tunnel across the English Channel, linking Europe to the UK.

The third reason why I propose suspending the project at this time is due to timing, both in terms of length of implementation and in terms of the timing of the necessary funding of the project. The U.S. rail system proposal will take years, if not decades, to implement and, more importantly, is only partially funded. As an example of the time involved, the Pennsylvania Project High Speed Maglev reports the following regarding the project to connecting Pittsburgh International Airport to Downtown and the east suburbs of Monroeville and Greensburg, a stretch of only forty to fifty miles. It is interesting to note that the selling points mentioned are the same stated by President Obama in his speech regarding the

U.S. HSR project, which are similar, to a tee, to those used to sell the Interstate Highway System to Americans some sixty years ago.

> Planning the next generation of high-speed ground transportation for Pennsylvania and the United States has been an ongoing activity for more than ten years.
>
> The project is not only about the planning for the deployment of the system in the U.S. It is also about the development of the private-public operating structure and organizations, innovative financing, development of the long term precision fabrication techniques required to construct the maglev guideway, and the vision on how this system will not only serve Pennsylvania, but our nation as it is expanded beyond the initial installation. We believe you will find that high-speed maglev is truly an ideal travel option for the 21st century. (Source: The Pennsylvania Project High Speed Maglev 2011)

Thirty one states have been selected to receive various levels of federal funding to implement the system. The majority of U.S. States are already at the brink of bankruptcy. The states of Ohio and Wisconsin, both slated for the expansion of the new rail system and substantial federal funding, are prime examples. "For the citizens of Ohio and Wisconsin, at least, this vision seems destined to remain in the realm of the imagination for some time to come. Despite the enticing picture painted by the president, the incoming Republican governors of those two states see nothing but red ink when they hear the phrase 'high speed rail'...both argue that the projects are expensive boondoggles and have vowed to scrap them, even though that will mean the loss of $400m in federal funding in Ohio's case, and $810m in Wisconsin's" (The Economist 2010c, 40).

The partial funding and reluctance of certain states to participate in the construction of a U.S. HSR is particularly relevant in highlighting one of the major inherent risks in this project, namely the enormous cost to construct the U.S. Maglev HSR system. Maglev describes the technology which is to be used in the U.S. system. Maglev stands for magnetic levitation. Magnetically levitated trains use the attracting and repelling forces of magnets as the pro-

Illustration 17. A View of the Shanghai Maglev System in Operation

Source: Shanghai Maglev Transportation Development Co., Ltd., 2011

pulsion force to run on specialized track systems. Below is a picture of the Chinese Shanghai Maglev system, the first high speed maglev system to be established commercially. Construction began in March 2001 and service was commenced on January 1, 2004. The line runs from Longyang Road station in Pudong to the Pudong International Airport. At full speed, the 30 km (19 mile) trip can be completed in 7 minutes and 20 seconds. The maglev can reach a speed of 350 km/h (220 mph) in 2 minutes. The top speed of 431 km/h (268 mph) is reached after two minutes of operation (Shanghai Maglev Transportation Development Co., Ltd., 2011). (See Illustration 17 above).

The cost of the construction of the Shanghai Maglev is estimated to have been over $1.2 billion for the 19 mile stretch. According to one source, "The system chews through $60 million a year in capital costs alone. Assuming 12,000 passengers a day, the maglev generates about $27 million of revenue a year, or less than half its capital costs, much less its total costs. It is not clear who is absorbing these losses" (Blodget 2005).

SBI Energy has provided an estimate of the costs for partial segments of the U.S. HSR system:

The U.S. is embracing Maglev HSR system for its future. The Maglev Deployment Program encourages the development and construction of an operating transportation system employing magnetic levitation, capable of safe use by the public at a speed in excess of 240 mph. The projected costs per mile of the Maglev systems are comparable to conventional electric light-rail systems when looked at in aggregate. The proposed Pennsylvania Maglev system, for example, is expected to cost more than $2.7 billion or $51.4 million per mile. The light-rail system proposed for Austin, Texas, in contrast, will also cost about $51 million per mile.

Of the two corridors in which Maglev shows favorable cost ratios, California is proposing to develop new HSR because of its ability to make flexible use of existing rail rights-of-way in densely-settled areas. The Northeast U.S. corridor has formidable environmental obstacles to the introduction of Maglev along much of its length, as well as other investment needs centering on the high-volume commuter and intercity rail passenger services that depend on the established and aging infrastructure. (SBI Energy 2011)

The example of the Shanghai maglev system and the SBI analysis regarding the proposed U.S. maglev high speed rail system highlight the fact that the costs are enormous. Further, the Shanghai maglev example also illustrates the financial risk involved - long amortization of capital cost and the consumption of resources. These resources represent the requisite cash infusion into the operations of the U.S. maglev high speed rail system to pay operating costs which may not be covered by revenues even at a high ticket price. Both of these points support my proposal to halt the project at this time of financial instability and uncertainty.

Two additional risks have been provided by the Shanghai example and the SBI analysis. The Shanghai project, from start of construction until commencement of service, was completed in less than three years. As noted above, the Pennsylvania project has been ten years in the making and is still not complete. The Shanghai project was driven by the highly centralized Chinese government. In the U.S., each of the fifty states is a single entity which acts independently. This is a major factor which could well impede the construction of a trans-national high speed rail system in the U.S., especially in consideration of the fact of the variable burden which will be placed on each state or region as a result of the existing infrastructure, as noted in the SBI analysis. For example, the Northeast region of the U.S. is dependent upon an established and aging infrastructure. In addition, considering the expansion range of the Administration's proposal, as aforementioned, the midsection of the nation is left without service. If the costs are significantly higher to implement the system in the Northeast with its aging infrastructure, I must ask why the costs and benefits of a true transnational system which spans virgin territory, which has no aging infrastructure, have not been taken into account.

The fourth reason why I propose the postponement of the construction of the high speed rail system in the U.S. at this time is the risk of consumer acceptance of this means of transportation, which has two aspects. First, we Americans are used to driving and consider the freedom of driving a right, as has been discussed. In addition, the cost/benefit of rail travel is not close to, yet alone superior, to travel by plane, as indicated in the above analysis of the travel parameters of a trip from Washington DC to Los Angeles. If the consumer does not fully embrace the high speed rail system as an acceptable and cost-effective mode of transportation, the risk of financial shortfall is certain. As seen in the case of the Shanghai high speed rail system, despite the high volume of traffic, estimated at over 12,000 passengers per day on the 19 mile stretch, the capital costs exceed the revenue generated. If the U.S. high speed rail system fails to attract sufficient passengers, operating costs would also be a threat to financial viability.

For these reasons, I recommend that the high speed interstate rail project, as presently proposed, be stopped immediately. Further, I propose that the financial and technical resources which were to be invested in that project be applied, in full measure, to the effort of making that mode of transportation which we have taken to full development, namely, the petroleum- fueled (gasoline and diesel versions) passenger car, as efficient as possible through the deployment of known technologies in new passenger vehicles within the next twenty four months with the effect that we will have truly contributed to reducing CO_2 emissions from passenger cars in the U.S. and also from the country as a whole. If, after this period, a well-defined program for the reengineering of U.S. passenger cars is in place and is actively being pursued, I would recommend that the high speed train project be reviewed. This project represents an important step forward in mobilizing America in an energy efficient manner, but the risks inherent in the project such as financing, length of implementation, financial status of the country and states, and acceptance by an individually motorized American consumer are great. This strategic project requires the proper place in time, such as that time during which the Interstate Highway System was planned and constructed, a time characterized by economic stability to enable and foster the cohesive and concerted action necessary to properly plan and implement the project.

The second transportation policy issue I address is the present Administration's singular support of electric vehicles. The 2012 budget released by the Obama Administration in February 2011 contained the following provision: $200 million in grants to thirty communities which advance electric vehicle use through fleet purchase, infrastructure and regulatory measures. The $200 million represents 72 percent of the total increase of $277 million to the Department of Energy's 2012 budget for spending on vehicle technologies. The present tax credit of $7,500 for buyers of electric vehicles would be transformed into an instant rebate at the dealership/point of purchase for the same amount, increasing the attractiveness to a prospective buyer in terms of immediate cash flow. In addition, the budget would eliminate all funds previously allocated for the development of hydrogen fuel cell technology, a sum of $49 million (Roland 2011, 8).

Before addressing the policy related issues, it is relevant to point out that there exist a plethora of definitions of what constitutes and electric vehicle. For the purpose of this discussion, the following categories, which reflect the most commonly accepted definitions of electric vehicle types, will be used.

Hybrid electric vehicles, such as the Toyota Prius and Ford Fusion Hybrid, use an electric motor in conjunction with a gasoline-powered internal combustion engine, providing increased fuel efficiency. These systems minimize idling and provide an integrated electric start and launch assist, which boosts the vehicle's ability to start and accelerate, which are important features for city driving. Both the electric motor and internal combustion engine are able to drive the wheels. The electric motor moves the vehicle from zero speed, such as from idle or stationary, up to minimal speeds which are generally less than 40 mph. The gas engine engages at higher speeds. The battery is recharged by regenerative braking, which uses the kinetic energy from the exertion of the brake pedal to charge the batteries. These vehicles are also known as parallel hybrids and power-split hybrids. Compared to other electric vehicles, these cars do not present range problems and do not need to be charged. They are more expensive than gasoline-powered internal combustion cars and also use gasoline, thereby producing CO_2 emissions.

Plug-in hybrid electric vehicles, like hybrid electric vehicles, are duel-fueled by a gasoline-powered internal combustion engine and batteries. The difference is that these electric vehicles can be plugged in to an electric outlet to extend the use of the battery as a means of propulsion. Like hybrids, these vehicles generally have a maximum speed of 40 mph for battery use and the gas powered engine engages at higher speeds. The gasoline engine also engages when the range of the battery has been reached. In addition, these vehicles are dependent on charging stations. These types of electric vehicles are also known as range-extended electric vehicles, plug-in hybrid electric vehicles (PHEV) or series hybrids. An example of this type of electric vehicle is the Chevy Volt. Like hybrid electric vehicles, plug ins do not present a range problem, but do require charging. And like hybrids, they use gasoline and produce CO_2 emissions, when the motor is engaged.

Vehicles which have no internal combustion engine and rely solely on batteries for propulsion are considered to be all electric vehicles and often referred to as Battery Electric Vehicles (BEVs) or pure electric vehicles. These vehicles require a larger battery pack to achieve an acceptable range and longer charging times, often requiring a 240 volt charge source. In the U.S., standard outlets are 120 volts. 240 volt outlets are in use for heavy-duty household equipment such as electric ranges. Examples of this full electric vehicle are the Nissan Leaf and the Mitsubishi i-MiEV. These vehicles produce no emissions but, as discussed, raise the questions of increased electrical power generation and a limited supply base.

Fuel cell vehicles are often classified as electric vehicles. In these electric vehicles, an onboard fuel cell uses hydrogen to generate electricity via a chemical reaction. They offer a range comparable to internal combustion engines, do not require petroleum-based fuel and emit only water. As aforementioned, the technology is extremely complex and at the present time, there is not infrastructure for the refueling of hydrogen- powered vehicles (Automotive News 2010).

As mentioned briefly, in Chapter III, the electric vehicle presents a major challenge, from a technological stand point, from an infrastructure standpoint, and from the important vista of the consumer. Presently, the main choice for powering electric passenger vehicles is a battery of a lithium composition, for three reasons. These batteries weigh significantly less than the traditional, readily available lead acid batteries, they are more compact and therefore require less packaging room in the vehicle, and they are more environmentally friendly. But that does not come without cost and risk.

At this time, lithium batteries are produced mainly in Asia, specifically China and South Korea. Import duties, lengthy transit time, the risk of currency fluctuations or shut down of the supply chain due to geopolitical issues are the main supply problems and the same problems which we now face with the fuel for gas powered engines due to our dependence on foreign oil. The present constellation of battery technology does not yet provide for adequate range and requires a substantial charging time. Both of these are major consumer issues. In addition, even if the range was increased, there is virtually no infrastructure in place to support the long range use of electric vehicles. Alternate battery technologies are being investigated, but these will take years to develop.

There are two inherent risks in relying on lithium batteries to automotive use – increasing and competing demand, and supply dependency. These were my main arguments regarding caution concerning the forced use of electric vehicles at all cost, and the use of lithium batteries, when I began this research early in 2010. Two major studies which were recently released, confirm my arguments.

The first is a study by the Department of Energy, *Critical Materials Strategy*, released in December, 2010 (DOE 2010). The second is a study chaired by Robert Jaffe undertaken by the American Physical Society Panel on Public Affairs and the Materials Research Society entitled, *Energy Critical Elements: Securing Material for Emerging Technologies*, released on February 18, 2011 (Jaffe et al 2011). I will use data from these reports as well as information which I obtained before the issuance of these most recent reports to present arguments to support my proposal to make a change in the present Administration's approach to electric vehicle technology.

In addition to use in automotive batteries, lithium is also used as a key component in rechargeable batteries for digital cameras, lap tops, and cell phones. The volume growth of these products which will compete with the lithium available for batteries for cars, is more likely to expand more rapidly and significantly then the growth of the electric vehicle market, thereby not only co-opting available lithium sources, but also driving prices higher. The BBC News reported that, in 2010, globally, there were over 5 billion mobile phones in use, and that more than 1 billion of these were added in the 18 months preceding July 2010. According to Ben Wood, a leading mobile phone analyst, that market is likely to explode in the future, due to the fact that people are, increasingly, owning multiple phones, especially in the developing countries where the mobile phone is often he only source of communication available, and is increasingly becoming integrated into daily life, as evidenced by the explosion of micro-financing to meet the commercial needs of daily life via cell phone. In addition, he notes, the increase in the use of connective devices such as USB dongles and the iPad will drive the growth (BBC 2010). The lithium demand for defense purposes, both domestic and foreign use, is undefined, but will certainly escalate as defense technologies become more dependent on battery technologies, adding yet another substantial demand factor for lithium.

A second risk in the reliance on lithium for automotive batteries is supply dependency, not just on certain nations, but on natural resources which may be available in limited quantities. According to the study by the American Physical Society, lithium (Li) is one of the Energy Critical Elements (ECE):

Li (atomic number 3, 0.002% of Earth's crust) is an example of an ECE whose future supply in the marketplace is experiencing significant uncertainty associate with time delays in production and utilization. Li, a light and highly reactive metal, is the principal component in one of the most promising forms of high energy-density batteries of choice for all-electric vehicles. If electric vehicles are to gain a significant share of the market, battery, and therefore Li production must grow proportionately. Ramping up the production of Li from existing mines and developing new ones is not a trivial matter, nor is the design of Li batteries suitable for all-electric vehicles. Lacking a clear decision on the fundamental battery design, it is not surprising that exploration for and development of new Li supplies remains in limbo. (Jaffe et al 2011, 11)

The DOE study identified the critical materials for certain clean energy technologies, such as wind turbines, electric vehicles, photovoltaic cells, and fluorescent lighting are dependent on materials which are at risk. These clean energy technologies presently

Illustration 18. Materials in Clean Energy Technologies and Components

		Solar Cells	Wind Turbines	Vehicles		Lighting
	MATERIAL	PV films	Magnets	Magnets	Batteries	Phosphors
Rare Earth Elements	Lanthanum				•	•
	Cerium				•	•
	Praseodymium		•	•	•	
	Neodymium		•	•	•	
	Samarium		•	•		
	Europium					•
	Terbium					•
	Dysprosium		•	•		
	Yttrium					•
	Indium	•				
	Gallium	•				
	Tellurium	•				
	Cobalt				•	
	Lithium				•	

Source: DOE 2010

account for about 20 percent of global consumption of the critical materials identified by the DOE, but as deployment increases rapidly, so will the share of use of these materials in these technologies grow. Eight of the fourteen critical materials identified by the DOE are necessary for the production of electric vehicle and are used in production of the magnets and the batteries, as shown in Illustration 18 (p. 100). Electric vehicles use electric traction motors to provide propulsion. Many electric and hybrid vehicle motors use neodymium permanent magnets (PMs) to improve the strength of the magnetic fields inside the motor to increase torque generation.

The DOE identified six rare earth elements which are most critical in the short term, 3 to 5 years: dysprosium, neodymium, terbium, europium, indium, and yttrium. Of these five critical elements, two are necessary for electric vehicle for use in magnets (dysprosium and neodymium) and batteries (neodymium). Dysprosium is ranked at the highest level of importance and also at the high-

Illustration 19. Critical Materials Ranked by Importance to Clean Technology and Rated According to Short-Term Supply Risk, 3-5 Years

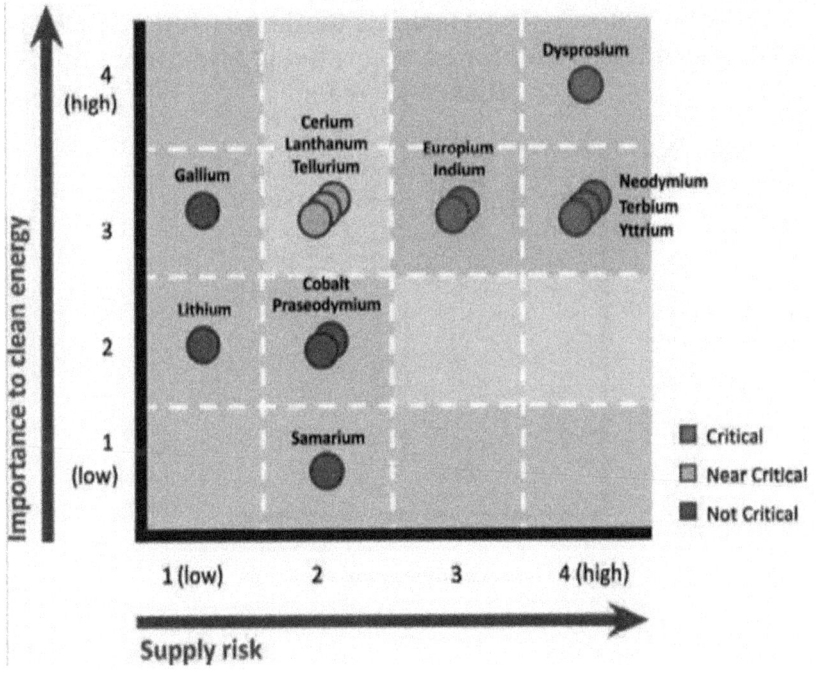

Source: DOE 2010

est level of supply risk in the short term of 3-5 years and is in the uppermost right quadrant. Like dysprosium, neodymium is also ranked in the highest quartile of supply risk and only slightly lower in the third quartile of importance to clean technologies. However, the importance of neodymium to electric vehicle technology is two-fold as it is a necessary element for the production of both batteries and magnets, as it be seen in Illustration 19 (p.101).

While four critical materials for electric vehicles are rated as low supply risk materials in the short term, namely lithium, cobalt, praseodymium, and samarium, two additional elements which are also critical for electric vehicle production are rated as near critical in the short term, cerium and lanthanum.

The situation changes dramatically and alarmingly in the mid-term outlook of 5 to 15 years. Neodymium, presently used both in magnets and batteries in electric vehicles, appears to be less of a supply risk, but becomes more critical as an important material for clean energy technologies. Lithium moves in an upward right diagonal and becomes not only more important to clean energy technologies, but is also at an increased supply risk, as can be seen below in Illustration 20.

Illustration 20. Critical Materials Ranked by Importance to Clean Technology and Rated According to Mid-Term Supply Risk, 5-15 Years

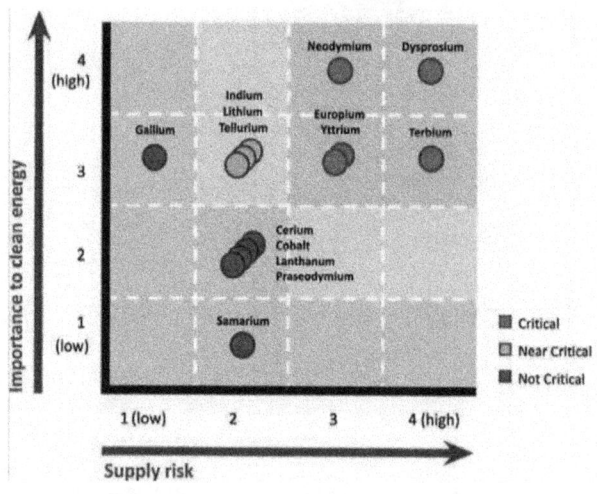

Source: DOE 2010

Similar to the situation we face with oil, increased use of lithium in U.S. electric vehicle batteries will also lead to a foreign dependency and possibly a reliance on fields where extraction and cleaning of the mineral lead to higher costs. "Global Li production is currently dominated by Chile....Bolivia also appears to have the potential for large Li resources" (Jaffe et al 2011, 11). Argentina could also a leading source. However, these sources and some new reported sources in Mexico may be of lower quality and costlier to develop than established sources. An additional risk is that countries with these minerals will protect them for national use. "The Salar de Atacama, the largest salt flat in Chile, is believed to contain the best quality lithium deposits, Chile is debating whether to allow more private companies to extract lithium or to protect the deposits for national business" (Rosenberg and Garcia 2011).

Both the issue of supply of lithium from, mainly, South America and the supply of lithium batteries, mainly from China and South Korea, present not only problems of foreign dependency but elevate the geopolitical risk of our dependency on foreign sources. This risk has been discussed regarding the situation with the unrest in the Mideast and our dependence on that region for some of our oil needs. In addition, "a recent report from the Department of Energy suggests that rare earth metals are a bigger supply concern. In the short term, the report does not find that lithium supply is likely to be an issue. After 2015, depending on the market penetration scenario for PHEVs and BEVs, demand does begin to outstrip potential supply (Hybridcars 2011b).

The availability of lithium is not the only critical issue with regard to this battery technology. Lithium battery technology is more complex due to the fact that there is no standard lithium battery and that the various versions of lithium batteries also require certain amounts of different elements. Lithium batteries, lithium ion (or Li-ion) batteries are important because they have a higher energy density - the amount of energy they hold by weight, or by volume - than any other type and can hold roughly twice as much energy per pound as do the previous generation of advanced batteries, nickel-metal-hydride (NiMH). It is this characteristic of lithium batteries which makes a feasible electric vehicle possible.

However, several different chemical formulations for the electrodes are in use, none of which is the perfect solution. In these batteries, the anode, or negative electrode, is typically made of graphite, but the cathode's, the positive electrode's, chemistry varies and the cathode material determines the battery cell's capacity. Cobalt dioxide is widely used in small cells, such as for cell phones. Presently, the only automotive application is in the Tesla Motors electric vehicle which uses over 6,000 cells and incorporates a liquid cooling system to safeguard against possible ignition between neighboring cells.

Nickel-cobalt-manganese (NCM) is somewhat easier to make. Manganese is cheaper than cobalt, but it dissolves slightly in electrolytes, leading to a shorter life.Substituting nickel and manganese for some of the cobalt allows manufacturers to tune the cell either for higher power (voltage) or for greater energy density, though not both at the same time.NCM remains susceptible to thermal loss, though less so than cobalt dioxide. Its long-term durability is still unclear, and nickel and manganese are both, at the present time, relatively expensive. Nickel-cobalt-aluminum (NCA) is similar to NCM, with lower-cost aluminum replacing the manganese.

Manganese oxide (MnO) offers higher power at a lower cost than cobalt, with the drawback of a much lower energy density. GS Yuasa, LG Chem, NEC-Lamilion Energy, and Samsung offer cells with such cathodes. LG Chem is the company which has joined forces with General Motors to produce lithium batteries for the GM Volt and is actively marketing to other companies.

Iron phosphate (FePo) is most likely the most promising cathode material, due to its stability and safety. Iron phosphate is inexpensive, and because the bonds between the iron, phosphate, and oxygen atoms are far stronger than those between cobalt and oxygen atoms, the oxygen is much harder to detach when overcharged. So if failure occurs, it does so without overheating. However, iron phosphate cells work at a lower voltage than cobalt, so more of them must be chained together to provide enough power to propel a motor. (Information partially obtained from Hybridcars 2008 and from personal knowledge).

General Motors has joined forces with LG of Korea via LG's U.S. subsidiary, LG Chem. Compact Power Inc. to provide lithium batteries for the present Chevy Volt electric plug in vehicle. On Jan. 6,

2011 General Motors and the U.S. Department of Energy's Argonne National Laboratory, "announced a global licensing agreement that allows GM to use Argonne-patented cathode material technology in its lithium-ion batteries for electrified vehicles. Argonne also licensed the technology to GM's incumbent battery-cell supplier, LG Chem, to manufacture and use in its Li-ion cells". The technology is being developed by UChicago Argonne LLC, a wholly owned laboratory management subsidiary of the University of Chicago. The new technology is expected to contribute to significant performance of lithium automotive batteries, including enabling charging at higher voltages which, in turn, increases energy storage capacity and increase battery life. LG Chem is also in discussion with Ford, Chrysler and several Chinese manufacturers regarding possible battery supply (Society of Automotive Engineers International 2011, 9).

At the Los Angeles Auto Show in November 2010, Toyota and Honda each presented a new electric vehicle which should be commercially available in 2012 and will be equipped with lithium batteries, the Toyota RAV4EV, a small SUV, and the Honda Fit, a subcompact car. Other companies have shown and announced the introduction of electric vehicles at recent auto shows. I cite the examples of Honda and Toyota for two reasons. First, these companies have no problem meeting the U.S. CAFE standards with their present vehicle offerings. In addition, executives from both of these leading companies were very cautious in speaking about the electric vehicle market. Honda expressed commitment to the market, but was careful to remark that, "this will be very much a customer-pulled program". Toyota also sees a role for electric vehicles, but estimates that that market will be "far, far below 10 percent" of the total market. Toyota sees the highest potential growth in the gas-electric hybrid segment (Dawson and Ramsey 2010). Gas-electric hybrid vehicles are also dependent on energy critical elements, as will be discussed, but are not so singularly dependent, as all-electric vehicles, on lithium battery technology.

The caution expressed by Honda and Toyota might serve them well. Considering the enormous investment General Motors and LG Chem are making in lithium battery technology, which in its present state is known to be less than optimal and costly, it may be the case that electric cars powered by lithium batteries will fall into the same technology lock-in and path dependency as the gas engine, and for the same reasons – high sunk costs and the substantial capital infusion which will be required for the development and establishment of the technology. This includes not only the investments of the automobile producers to design, develop and produce the vehicles, but also of the government, at all levels and private providers to establish an infrastructure for charging electric vehicles. This could well create a situation in which other truly energy efficient alternative technologies, such as fuel cells, air and solar-powered vehicles remain on the sidelines due to technological lock in and path dependency on plug-in electric vehicles.

Although, as noted above, Toyota executives expressed caution about an aggressive entrance into the electric vehicle market, it is interesting to note two recent moves by Toyota. In January 2011, the company announced that future generation hybrid vehicles will no longer be powered by nickel metal hydride batteries, which do not compare with lithium batteries in terms of performance, reliance and space requirements, but by lithium batteries (Miller 2011). It is also interesting to note that, according to Reuters, "a sister company of Toyota Motor Corp. agreed with Australia's Orocobre Ltd. in January [2010] to jointly develop a $80 - $100 million lithium project at Argentina's Olaroz salt lake" (Rosenberg and Garcia 2010). By the next model year, 2012, electric vehicles of all types in the U.S. will rely almost exclusively on lithium batteries.

One other important factor concerning the use of electric vehicles, which is often overlooked, is the availability of sufficient electricity, should the vehicles be accepted and the use of them become wide-spread. Coal is presently the main source of electricity production in the U.S. According to the Edison Electric Institute, from 2000 to 2008, construction was begun on twenty new coal-fired units in nineteen plants. Since then, there has been no new construction of a single coal-fired power plant in the U.S. In 2010, utilities and power companies dropped plans to construct 38 new plants and retire 45 aging or inefficient plants, according to the Sierra Club. However, the federal Energy Information Administration estimates the 30 to 40 new plants will be required across the nation to be able to supply the 21 gigawatts of new electricity demand in

2035. (Mufson 2011a, G5). If sufficient natural gas and other sources of electricity generation plants, such as nuclear, wind and solar, are not available, the supply of electricity may fall much short of demand.

It must also be noted, that the construction of electric plants which use alternate sources is a complex multi-faceted undertaking. Problems range from the substantial investment required to construct and operate these plants, the type of fuel used, i.e. enriched uranium for nuclear plants which has a potential risk of radiation exposure, natural gas plants with the risk of explosion, and wind turbines which are dependent on sufficient wind energy to be run efficiently. In addition, these alternate energy power plants are likely to meet with resistance from the communities in which they are to be constructed, blocked by people who do not want to live next to a nuclear facility or have their view of the landscape marred by wind- powered generators or solar collectors.

Despite a lack of infrastructure for refueling of hydrogen powered vehicles and fuel cell technology, almost all major automobile producers are intending to enter into the market around the 2015 timeframe. These vehicles require neither gasoline nor electricity from an external source and also produce no emissions. According to Kranz ,"The push for fuel cells is also fueled by the realization by automakers that the hybrid, the plug-in hybrid and battery-powered vehicles collectively will be unable to meet stiffer CO_2 regulations later this decade" (Kranz 2010b, 20J).

Another, and potentially the greatest risk regarding the rapid and one-sided deployment of the electric vehicle is the aspect of consumer acceptance. At this time, it appears to be highly unlikely that electric vehicles will be embraced by the consumer at large. As Keith Crain, Editor of *Automotive News* and well-known automotive analyst, notes, "Electric cars, hybrids and other types of electric-powered vehicles will play a part in the mix of propulsion systems that power the cars of tomorrow. But the idea that electric cars will account for a major share of the market is wildly optimistic" (Crain 2010, 12). "In the next half-century we will see more and more electric vehicles. But not for a while - not until the economics make sense to lots of customers. Electric vehicles don't yet make economic sense" (Crain 2011, 12).

Crain also reiterates the overarching importance of the economic considerations of manufacturers as well as consumers, "In the next 25 years, petroleum will still have the lion's share of powerplants, [engines in automotive jargon], whether it's diesel or gasoline. After more than 100 years we have too much invested worldwide to replace the entire infrastructure in the space of a few decades. It's not going to happen...A number of fuels will be used in the next 50 years, but to assume that most propulsion systems are going to be electric is misleading....There are too many people in the government who are in love with electric vehicles....There will be a place in the mix of propulsion systems in the future for electric cars. But it will be a modest amount that makes the most sense in certain settings. Anyone who plans for more than that is in for a rude awakening" (Crain 2010, 12).

For these reasons – risks of supply and availability of sufficient natural resources, the lack of an infrastructure and enormous cost to construct one, the risk of technology-lock in and path dependency, as well as the high unknown factor of consumer acceptance of electric vehicles, I propose that all federal and state investments in the present electric vehicle technology which relies on lithium and other battery technologies and the construction of an infrastructure for these vehicles be halted and reinvested as described in the following proposal, the U.S. Clean Car Program. We cannot afford to become path dependent on yet another technology which is already moving rapidly towards that destiny and which is not well defined, as evidenced by the many solutions available, and especially because the fuel source, both the battery technology and the lithium supply are presently under the control of a few foreign suppliers which are located in areas of geopolitical risk.

The funding which the present Administration has allocated exclusively to the development of electric cars and a supporting infrastructure, should be channeled into the effort to make existing passenger cars, for which we have proven viable and available technical environmental friendly solutions and which are accepted by the consumer, and for which we have an existing and solid infrastructure, to support the short term upgrade of existing vehicles which already meet CAFE standards. Thereafter, remaining funding should be dedicated to investigate truly environmentally safe vehicle propulsion systems such as hydrogen and air fuel cells as well as solar powered vehicles. I am not suggesting that the government control the investment of private companies in electric vehicle or battery technology. Rather, I am proposing that the playing field be leveled and that we take the most doable practical and pragmatic approach available to us towards making as many passenger cars, upon which we will continue to rely for quite a while, as environmentally friendly and emissions free as possible to effect a very short term impact on rising CO_2 levels due to passenger cars emissions in the U.S.

Third, I propose a further leveling of the play field in the form of an increase of tax on gasoline at the federal level. In the U.S., tax is levied on fuels for passenger cars in various forms and at different levels. An analysis of fuel surcharges at the state and local levels revealed that the state tax varied greatly between states and concerning the tax levied on gasoline and diesel fuel. Gasohol blends are taxed at the same rate as gasoline in all states and the District of Columbia. (Note: Although not politically accurate, the word state in this discussion will include the District of Columbia for the ease of discussion). At the Federal level, diesel is burdened with a tax which is over 23 percent higher than the tax on gasoline. At the state level, on the average, the difference is about 2 percent. These numbers include excise tax, environmental taxes, special taxes but are exclusive of county and local taxes. States which do not appear in this table tax all fuels at the same rate in terms of cents per gallon.

The fuel prices for gasoline and diesel highlighted in Table 17 indicate that the prices in these states are higher than the national average for each of these fuels, 22.44 and 22.95 cents per gallon, respectively. When only state taxes are considered, it can be seen that the states of Connecticut and Florida levy significantly higher taxes on diesel fuel than on gasoline, 36.9 percent and 45.9 percent, respectively. Conversely, the states of California and Michigan tax diesel at a much lower rate than gasoline. The rate of taxation for diesel fuel in California is over 96 percent below the tax levied on gasoline. When the total tax rate, federal and state combined, is considered the situation changes dramatically, indicating the leverage effect of the federal tax. Of those states which tax diesel fuel at a lower rate than gasoline, only California shows a slight advantage for diesel versus gasoline when the total tax burden, federal and state tax is considered. In effect, the diesel advantage of over 96 percent in California is reduced by two-thirds through the levy of federal taxes on diesel fuel. While this analysis may not be complete in every detail, and certain additional taxes and levies at state and local levels exist and are not included here due to the pure number of these taxes and charges which would have made any further degree of accuracy difficult to ensure, it is based on the latest fuel tax data from the EIA as of March 2011 and can serve as a basis for my proposal, as shown in Table 17.

Table 17. Federal and State Motor Fuel Taxes - 2011 (cents per gallon)

	Motor Gasoline	Diesel	Diff. Diesel to Gasoline (%)	Motor Gasoline (State and Fed. Tax)	Diesel (State and Fed. Tax)	Diff. Diesel to Gasoline (%)
Federal	18.40	24.00	23.3%			
Avg. State Tax	22.44	22.95	2.2%			
Alabama	18.00	21.00	14.3%	36.40	45.00	19.1%
Alaska	8.00	8.00	0.0%	26.40	32.00	17.5%
Arizona	18.00	18.00	0.0%	36.40	42.00	13.3%
Arkansas	21.50	22.50	4.4%	39.90	46.50	14.2%
California	35.30	18.00	-96.1%	53.70	42.00	-27.9%
Colorado	22.00	20.50	-7.3%	40.40	44.50	9.2%
Connecticut	25.00	39.60	36.9%	43.40	63.60	31.8%
Delaware	23.00	22.00	-4.5%	41.40	46.00	10.0%
DC	23.50	23.50	0.0%	41.90	47.50	11.8%
Florida	16.00	29.60	45.9%	34.40	53.60	35.8%
Georgia	7.50	7.50	0.0%	25.90	31.50	17.8%
Hawaii	17.00	17.00	0.0%	35.40	41.00	13.7%
Idaho	25.00	25.00	0.0%	43.40	49.00	11.4%
Illinois	19.00	21.50	11.6%	37.40	45.50	17.8%
Indiana	18.00	16.00	-12.5%	36.40	40.00	9.0%
Iowa	21.00	22.50	6.7%	39.40	46.50	15.3%
Kansas	24.00	26.00	7.7%	42.40	50.00	15.2%
Kentucky	24.50	21.50	-14.0%	42.90	45.50	5.7%
Louisiana	20.00	20.00	0.0%	38.40	44.00	12.7%
Maine	29.50	30.70	3.9%	47.90	54.70	12.4%
Maryland	23.50	24.25	3.1%	41.90	48.25	13.2%
Massachusetts	21.00	21.00	0.0%	39.40	45.00	12.4%
Michigan	19.00	15.00	-26.7%	37.40	39.00	4.1%
Minnesota	27.50	27.50	0.0%	45.90	51.50	10.9%
Montana	27.00	22.95	-17.6%	45.40	46.95	3.3%

Above State Avg.
Diesel taxed than Gas
Diesel taxed more than Gas

Source: EIA 2011d

As discussed in previous chapters, diesel engines are much more efficient than gasoline-powered engines; however diesel technology tends to be more expensive. For example, in the U.S., a Volkswagen 2011 Jetta sedan with a gasoline-powered engine carries a sticker price of $15,995 for the base model. The base model 2011 Jetta sedan equipped with a TDI turbo-diesel engine has a MSRP (Manufacturer's Suggested Retail Price) of $ 22,995, which is $7,000 more than the MSRP of the gasoline version. However, the TDI is rated at 30/42 mpg city/highway while the gasoline version is rated at 24/34 mpg city/highway (Volkswagen 2011).

As previously discussed, diesel-powered vehicles represent over half of the European market because of tax advantages. The same holds true for small cars in Japan, which are incentivized by the government, as has been discussed. Given that small cars might not be a viable option for the majority of American drivers at this time, and given that we need to make a swift change to get passenger vehicles on the road with improved fuel economy which leads to lower emissions using available technology and the infrastructure we have, I propose the following. The analysis presented above shows that the real lever in total fuel tax is at the federal level. It also shows that diesel fuel is taxed at a rate of 5.60 cents per gallon higher than gasoline. A simple, straightforward calculation using the data in the above Table indicates that if that difference of 5.60 cents per gallon were applied to the gasoline tax at the federal level, increasing the tax rate to that of the levy on diesel fuel at the federal level, the average total increase in gasoline fuel price across all states would be about 13 percent. The real leverage to get diesel technology on the road and discourage the continued use of gas guzzlers is that the "new" gas total tax burden would be only slightly higher than diesel, some 0.1percent, and that the playing field would be leveled. This would encourage the consumer to consider the purchase of a diesel vehicle and also would more evenly spread the cost of fuel among vehicles types, including hybrid vehicles. The increased revenues to the Federal government from the higher tax on gasoline should be used, initially, to fund the $1,000 Clean Car incentive and thereafter, to fund the development of new passenger vehicle technologies as will be presented in the sections following the presentation proposal regarding CAFE standards.

The fourth measure is, perhaps, less of a policy measure than of a tactical nature and concerns CAFE standards. It has been shown in Chapter III, via an analysis of present efficiency rankings that certain passenger car models and the light truck models of the Big Three fall short of the 2012 targets, it has also been discussed that substantial engineering effort is being invested to attempt to re-engineer these models to meet the new standards. It must be noted that these models are those which are most preferred by the U.S. consumer, as ranked by sales volume.

As previously mentioned, that the EPA and the NHTSA consulted with, among others, the automobile producers when developing the new CAFE standards. However, even as recently as January 2011, General Motors and Chrysler which are still partially owned by the U.S. government after the 2009 bail outs have joined a coalition to lobby against the proposed fuel efficiency rulings. As Ralph Nader, well known crusader for consumer rights and automobile activist, states, "Even when the government owned 61 percent of General Motors, the company was arguing against government proposals on auto safety and pollution controls. As the owner of the world's second largest auto company, the government could have made the company a model". It didn't in Nader's view. "It's hard to make something like this up" (Whoriskey 2011a, A17). The government owned 61 percent of General Motors until November of 2010 when its stake was reduced to 33 percent after the public stock offering. The government still owns 9 percent of Chrysler (Whoriskey 2011a, A17).

Yet another example of the need to reign in the industry and not allow the proliferation of those vehicles which fail to meet the CAFE standards is the introduction of Mahindra's pickup in the U.S. Mahindra & Mahindra Ltd. of India have developed a franchise system of some 350 dealers in the U.S. to sell its 4 cylinder pickup truck, which was initially announced to deliver 30 mpg. The truck's official EPA rating is 19/21 city/highway, slightly above the Ford F150. It has been shown in Chapter III that that U.S. light truck CAFE standard in 2012 is 25.7 mpg and for 2013, 26.4 mpg. The Mahindra truck is far from meeting these standards. However, prospective dealers are still looking forward to selling the vehicles despite the fact that the initial efficiency promised by Mahindra has not been met and also that the trucks fall short of CAFE standards. One of these enthusiastic dealers is quoted in *Automotive News*, "It's obviously disappointing and I'd like to know why it's different from what they promised....But I'm not going to drop the franchise. It's still a viable product and I'm looking forward to selling it" (Chappell 2011, 6).

As has been shown in Chapter III, in the past, regulators at the federal level have backed off on CAFE standards in deference to automobile producers and the oil industry. This can no longer be the case. As has also been discussed, the new CAFE standards are weak, when compared with other developed nations. There can be neither slippage nor exception. There is no excuse for not achieving and enforcing these rather lax standards, given the available technology. A further relaxation of the standards would indicate that the government is catering to specific industry players and has no definitive interest in reducing CO_2 emissions from passenger vehicles.

This leads to the next initiative, the refurbishment of existing passenger vehicles in the U.S.

The U.S. Clean Car Program

This discussion will continue with some of the technologies introduced in Chapter III which can be deployed in U.S. passenger vehicles to meet present and future CAFE standards with the goal, as discussed above, of exercising a concerted and immediate effort to reduce CO_2 emissions from U.S. passenger cars in the most pragmatic and practical manner possible – through the use of existing and readily available technology. Two areas will be briefly considered, transmission and engine technology. Selected technologies of certain manufacturers will be used to highlight the features of these technologies. This does not imply that these companies are the sole sources of the technologies or the leading manufacturers, nor is the selection of a certain manufacturer intended to promote that company.

The CVT (Continuously Variable Transmission), unlike conventional transmission systems which use fixed gears, provides for a smooth step up and step down to change gear rations. The CVT is an automatic transmission which uses two pulleys with a steel belt running between them. In order to continuously vary its gear ratios, the CVT simultaneously adjusts the diameter of the drive which transmits torque from the engine and the driven pulley which transfers torque to the wheels. According to the U.S. Department of Energy, present CVT systems offer an efficiency improvement of 6 percent over comparable vehicles without CVT technology which translate into a savings of some $1,600 in fuel cost saving over the life of the vehicle, assuming an average lifetime of 185,000 miles and an average fuel cost of $3.07 with an average fuel economy of 21 mpg (DOE 2011).

Nissan, a leader in introducing CVT technology, will be introducing its new generation XTRONIC CVT globally to reduce weight, size and increase fuel economy. The new CVT is targeted to reduce internal friction by 30 percent, weight by 13 percent and size by 10 percent as compared with the present Nissan CVT in the same vehicle class. This will lead to an additional 10 percent increase in fuel efficiency (Nissan 2011). (See Illustration 21)

Illustration 21. Nissan's Next Generation CVT

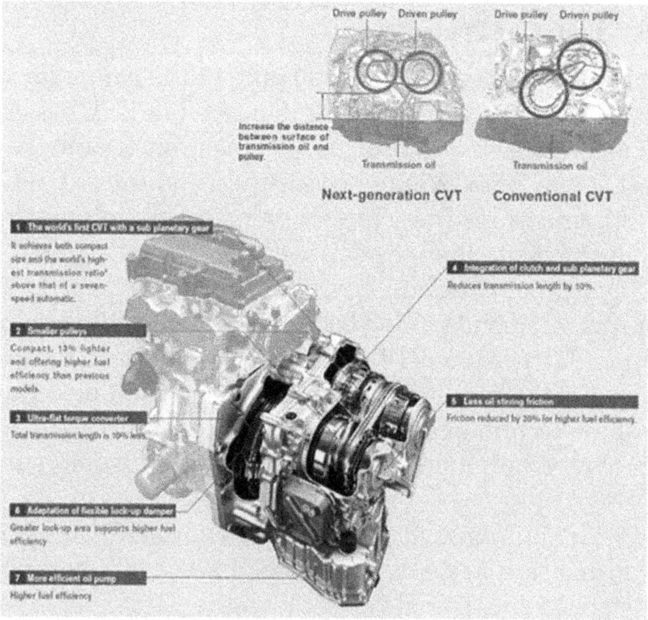

Source: Nissan 2011

Another transmission technology which is key to increasing fuel economy is the dual clutch transmission. The company LuK developed the technology, both in its conventional wet, i.e. hydraulic, and the newest dry, i.e. non-hydraulic form. The system combines the comfort of a conventional automatic planetary transmission with the efficiency of a manual transmission. It consists of two clutches which are arranged on two different drive shafts. One clutch is used for the uneven gears, while the second clutch controls the disengaging and engaging of the even gears and the reverse gear. During acceleration in second gear, for example, the third gear stage in the other sub-transmission is already preselected. As a result, the gear is shifted in a space of milliseconds without interrupting the tractive force. Control is carried out electronically and gearshifts are performed by means of hydraulic actuators, as shown in Illustration 22, p. 117 (LuK 2011).

In comparison to the wet double-clutch solution, in which the torque is transmitted between the disks via oil, in the dry clutch the friction lock-up is achieved using the friction linings of the clutch disks. "The elimination of the hydraulic support systems and the high efficiency of the dry clutch enables significant savings in fuel consumption of more than 10 percent in comparison to the wet clutch and up to 6 percent in comparison to manual transmissions. The potential for reducing CO_2 is between 12 and 18 percent in comparison to conventional automatic transmissions" (LuK 2011). (See Illustration 23, p. 117).

Diesel powered vehicles also offer a significant advantage over those vehicles powered by gasoline engines. Diesel engines are more powerful and are up to 35 percent more fuel-efficient than similar-sized gasoline engines. In the past, the diesel has offered less comfort than the gas powered vehicle but these issues have been resolved. Improved fuel injection and electronic engine control technologies have increased power as well as acceleration and fuel economy. The present day diesels are quieter than in the past and the past problems of cold weather start have been resolved. Through the use of low sulfur diesel fuel, diesel powered vehicles offer a cleaner ride than their gas competitors in terms of CO_2 emissions (DOE 2011).

Variable valve timing and variable lift systems, as well as cylinder deactivation were briefly mentioned in Chapter III as engine technologies which improve the fuel efficiency of gasoline engines. The Schaeffler Group, in cooperation with Fiat has developed and brought to production a system which combines these technologies and can be deployed in both gasoline and diesel engines. The UniAir valve control system, which made its debut in the Alfa MiTo 1.4 MultiAir, will be introduced in the U.S. in 2011 in the Fiat 500.

The fully-variable valve control system reduces fuel consumption and CO_2 emissions up to 25 percent. In addition, other emissions are also greatly reduced, hydrocarbons by some 40 percent and nitrogen oxide emissions (NOx) up to 60 percent. The system, dubbed UniAir by Schaeffler is named MultiAir by Fiat. "UniAir is a cam-actuated, electro-hydraulic valve train system. The fully-variable valve control system can be used in both gasoline and diesel engines and is supplied via the existing engine oil circuit. UniAir allows the implementation of throttle-free, continuously variable, software-based load control in gasoline engines across the entire engine operating map. In diesel engines, it enables the regulation of the combustion chamber temperature by means of a precise control of exhaust gas recirculation rates. At the same time, the effective compression ratio in the cylinder can be varied so as to ensure a homogeneous combustion... For the first time, this fully-variable valve control system allows not only variations in the valve lift, but also multiple opening and closing valve events at different intervals during a cycle. Thus, UniAir significantly expands the potential of previous variable valve control mechanisms" (Schaeffler Group 2011).

The joint development was initiated in 1999 and formalized in 2000. Production began in 2009, highlighting the long development time to market for many new, complex technologies. (See Illustration 24, p. 118).

This overview highlights some of the leading technologies which are available and which significantly contribute to the reduction of CO_2 emissions and the increase in fuel economy of passenger cars. It is therefore, that I propose that automobile producers work towards the purpose of defining definite paths of introduction of such readily available technologies into those passenger cars which fail to meet future CAFE standards and are presently not making

Peril or Promise 117

Illustration 22. Dual Clutch Basic Functional Diagram

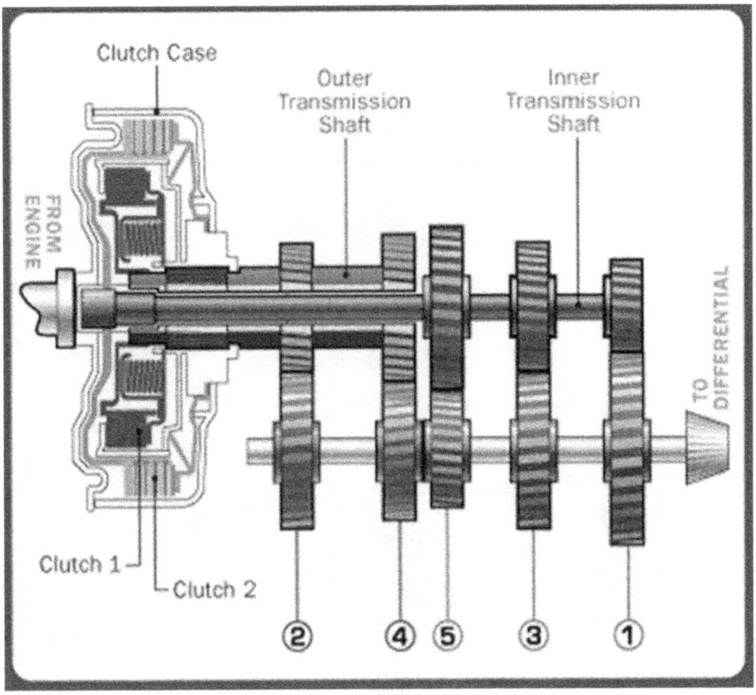

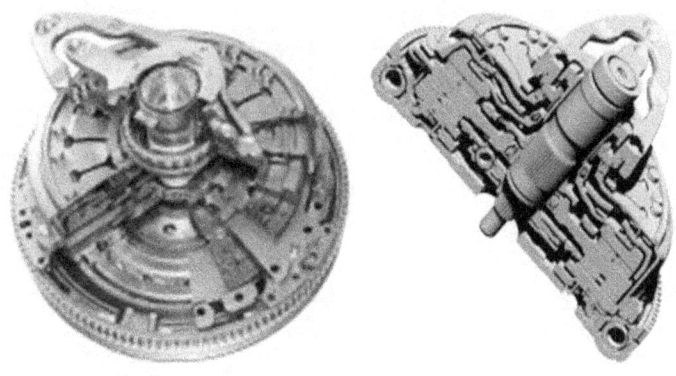

Source: Autoblog 2011

Illustration 23. The LuK Dry Clutch in Two Views

Side View

Cross Section
showing the two clutches

Source: Schaeffler Group 2008

Illustration 24. The Schaeffler UniAir System

Source: Schaeffler Group 2010

use of such technologies. This is not to support any particular supplier of these technologies or to promote shared corporate ownership. Licensing and cross-licensing agreements, if required, can be arranged and are standard practice in the automotive industry.

In addition, I proposed that, given the central motivation of economics in the passenger car system, that rather than offering a rebate of $7,500 for an all electric vehicle, the government offer a customer rebate of $1,000 at the point of purchase on all vehicles which meet or exceed the CAFE standards and which incorporate these new technologies in one form or another, as well as electric vehicles. Rather than offering an expensive incentive for a limited number of vehicles, i.e. electric vehicles which are available in limited quantities and which, as has been discussed, do not really solve the environmental problem, a broad based initiative such as my proposal would draw the attention of the consumer to new technologies and provide an incentive to purchase a vehicle which employed that technology. This proposal would also put the onus on the automobile producers who have failed to introduce available technologies to do so. The market would then not be slanted towards the electric vehicles which have performance issues which fail to meet consumer needs, such as range and real infrastructure problems as charging station. Key is that, in the face of rising gas prices, an overall increased burden on the economy due to rising oil and food prices, perhaps a true market picture would come into view, without one-sided subvention of electric vehicles and with the fair reward to those customers who purchase a vehicle which meets the governmental standards.

The point is that unless such an initiative is undertaken, we will not leverage to the fullest extent possible the investment we have made in a known technology and upon which we are dependent, namely passenger vehicles which are powered with petroleum-based products. While this is not the optimal solution to reducing CO_2 emissions from passenger vehicles in the U.S., I submit that it is the only solution which is achievable in the short term with a measure of certainty and predictability.

The further investment in full electric and hybrid vehicles is fraught with risk. The situation regarding full electric vehicles has already been discussed. And while hybrid vehicles rely on regenerative braking to power the batteries they carry to drive without using the gasoline powered engine under optimal conditions, these vehicles are still reliant on lithium batteries. It has been shown that the reliance on lithium as a power source is laden with risk due to more prominent and growing technologies which require lithium for batteries and will compete for the supply of that element, such as cell phones and computers. Further, it has been shown that the possible recriminations of geopolitical disturbances and dependence on a foreign source for the supply of lithium are inherent risks. In addition, the high strength magnets used in hybrid vehicles are dependent on sufficient supply of energy critical elements such as, dysprosium, geranium, indium, selenium, silver and tellurium.

If we can focus our efforts in the short term on deploying existing technologies in the present passenger vehicle fleet and retire those vehicles which have no hope of achieving the CAFE standards, a significant step will have been taken to reduce CO_2 emissions from passenger vehicles. However, as highlighted above, new technologies which have yet to be fully developed and proven will need to be introduced to eliminate the negative impact of passenger car travel on human health. This is an endeavor which will require intense cooperation between the automobile manufacturers, suppliers and research institutions to identify those technologies which are viable, manageable and can be implemented in the midterm.

Creation and Implementation of Sharing of Technology for the Environment Program (STEP)

The magnitude of technological change required to engineer and expediently deploy passenger vehicles which are not reliant on fossil fuels and do not contribute to rising CO_2 emissions is enormous. Intercompany and sector cooperation is essential to achieve any progress towards defining, let alone realizing new technologies which contribute to real progress towards flattening and which can lead both to improved fuel economy and a reduction in GHG emissions in the form of CO_2 from passenger cars. However, as has been discussed, the passenger car sector is not a lone entity in the future arena of energy needs and demands, and the supply of those resources necessary to meet those demands while reducing CO_2 emissions.

I therefore, recommend a twofold approach to the technology aspect. First, that the presidential task force, as mentioned in the previous chapter, also be charged with the goal of defining realizable solutions for passenger cars which are commensurate with the available resources and which no longer contribute to rising CO_2 emissions. This will entail a review of all technologies in the pipeline and an evaluation of those which are viable in consideration of how these impact the earth and human beings in two ways: the emissions scenarios and the availability of the earth's resources to produce these technologies. For example, solar and air fuel cell vehicles have been popularized as zero emissions vehicles, which is true. However, these vehicles rely heavily on the supply of certain elements which are rare and the quantities of which are unknown and are also being incorporated rapidly into non-vehicle techno-

Peril or Promise   121

logical developments, such as solar panels, thin solar films, and advanced power systems.

These elements are also increasingly being incorporated into new defense technologies, however the consumption for this purpose is not publicly recorded. Yet, as recently as February 2011 it has been reported the U.S. is urged to safeguard the supply of certain of these elements, not only for use in new technologies such as electric cars, wind turbines and solar cells, but also to ensure the availability for use in certain products critical to national defense (Vastag 2011, A6). (See Illustration 25 on the following page).

The above illustration identifies these critical elements. Not only is lithium (Li no. 3) identified as an energy critical element, and as previously discussed, is already known to be supply constrained in certain regions which may carry geopolitical risks, but many other elements integral to new innovations such as solar powered vehicles and fuel cells are also considered to be critical. Of particular concern are the rare earth elements (REE), shown above in purple. As noted by the American Physical Society, "The present concentration of REE production in China is a particularly pertinent example [of foreign dependency on these elements]...Although the United States led the world in both production and expertise into the 1990s, over 95 % of these important elements are now produced in China, and China is rapidly becoming the center for RRE extraction and processing expertise. Even if natural resources exist in a country, a lack of expertise and extraction, refining, and processing infrastructure can significantly influence international trade of ECEs, as is now the case with REEs" (Jaffe et al 2011, 5).

The goal of the proposed task force will be to identify and define those vehicle technologies which are the least reliant on any resource. This may well mean that future effort will need to be devoted to the development of hydrogen and air powered vehicles which are powered by highly compressed gases. I have no concrete proposal regarding the technology but am providing a direction which may be the only true path to fossil fuel independence and a reliable source of transportation which does not impact human health.

This will meet with resistance from companies that possess the technologies which will argue that they have paid the devel-

Illustration 25. The Periodic Chart - Energy Critical Elements (Source: Jaffe et al 2011)

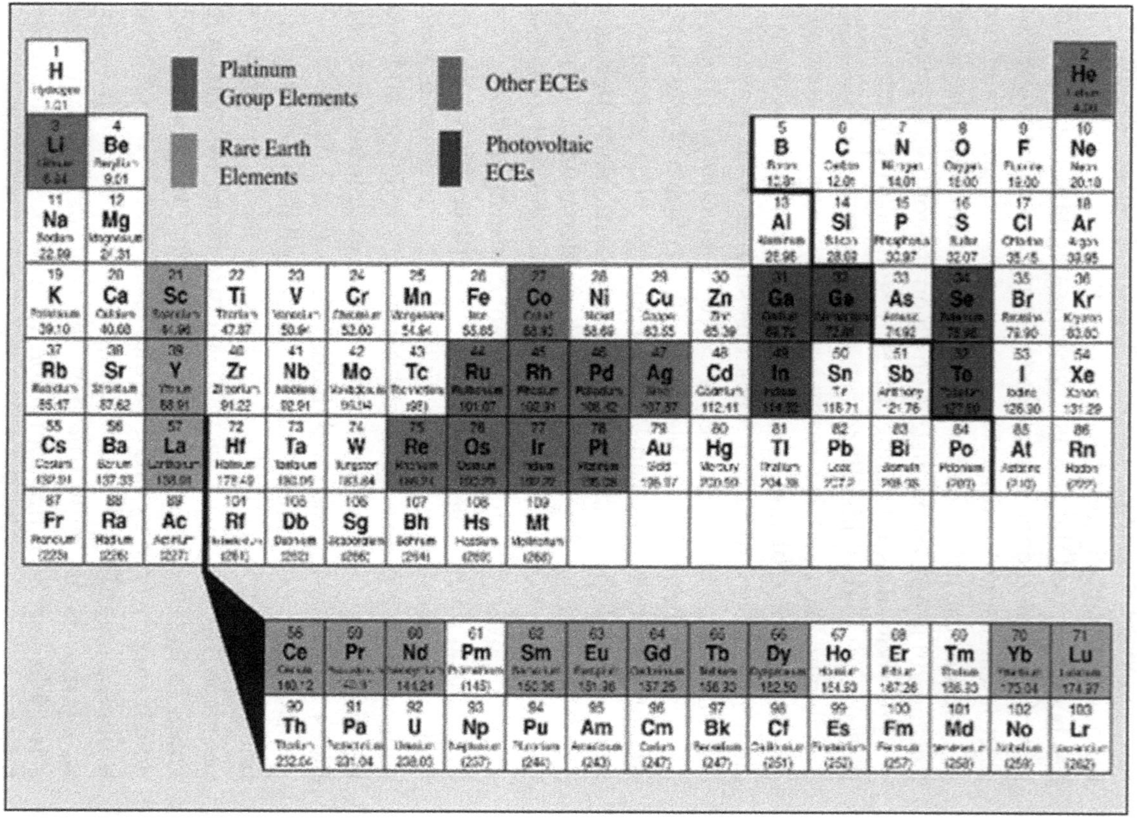

Source: Jaffe et al 2011

opment of these. This issue will need to be dealt with, up front. Governments and existing agencies that believe that this is within their jurisdiction will also be resistant to this effort. However, the coordinated and combined effort to share technology and deploy environmentally friendly products as expediently as possible is an important step in helping our country to manage the present situation, in an attempt to save the future.

Rycroft highlights the need for learning by interaction to foster the development of complex technologies, such as those which will be needed to help overcome our reliance on fossil fuels. He also speaks of the hindrance our present market driven competitiveness to not share technology imposes. "Markets left unfettered except for incentives to compete have trouble coping with cooperative learning dynamics that are a t the core of innovation of complex technologies....Complex learning involves substantial coordination, because investments must be made in different activities, often in different sectors" (Rycroft 2003, 2). He maintains that "accessing tacit knowledge...and integrating it with codified knowledge is strength of many networks which can reorganize themselves into more complex structures" (Rycroft 2003, 1).

Establishment and Completion of Project to Define Environmental Economic Metrics for the U.S.

The topic of cost benefit analysis has been addressed throughout this discussion, from the opening argument for the Kantian *sui generis* duty in which I stated that our society and our politics are highly influenced by incrementalism and logical positivism and, in line with Sagoff, that we tend to want to reduce all decisions to a type of data-based decision or a cost-benefit analysis (Sagoff 1998, 330). In Chapter II, I demonstrated that we have traded the benefits of health and that of future generations for the cost of cheap fuel and the luxury of driving. In Chapter III, I showed that this is a result of a complex interplay of relations and motivations between the participants in the U.S. passenger car sector and that, additionally; there is an emotional component which has become embedded in our American psyche – freedom in the form of unlimited and uninhibited mobility. Throughout the complete discussion, however the terms cost and benefits have been omnipresent.

As mentioned in Chapter I, Sagoff posits that when we use the market model as the basis of all decisions, we are "ignoring competing visions of what a society should be like" (Sagoff 1998, 334) and manage society as a market in which individuals trade freely and in which there is no central authority – neither a particular individual person, belief, or faith. He maintains that we cannot replace moral law with economic analysis because "the antinomianism of cost-benefit analysis is not enough" (Sagoff 1998, 334). Yet, it has been shown that we in the U.S. are driven by this concept which is so imbued in our society and in our calculations of what we do, purchase, invest in or spend our time. So, in conclusion, I propose that we need to find a way to bring this situation in line with a model which can actively promote environmental sustainability, while respecting the value of a an individual's life, regardless of his economic position. This is the content of my final proposal for a midterm solution. This is a lofty, but necessary goal. We can only continue to patch together progress toward the acceptance of environmentally friendly vehicles in the form of subsidies and rebates for a very limited time.

Ultimately, and soon, the U.S. will have to take its stance with regard to environmental economic metrics in the global arena. This will be a contentious project which will require years to resolve. It is, therefore, that I maintain that we must act now, in our own interest, as a community and a nation to also move this aspect of environmental concern forward by developing a set of national econometrics for environmental aspects. These will, in the first instance, be neither perfect nor all-inclusive. But it will be a beginning, and a necessary and difficult birth. As long as our focus remains on economics, we will have to find a way to fairly measure all goods, services, and aspects across the value chain in these terms if we are to promote any measure of environmental impact beyond the technological and other proposals I have made in this thesis.

This is not inconsistent with my arguments presented in Chapter I with regard to the Kantian *sui generis* duty to provide for those resources necessary for human life to flourish for all humans irrespective of their place in time. I do not propose that we place a value on life, but rather on the commodities which we use to maintain life, and not just those which go into or come out of production, but all of those which are consumed and affected by the production of any good.

I am certainly not the first to propose the need for such metrics or the concept that all steps in the value chain must be considered. There have been many more expert than me who have addressed this issue. And therefore, I will not delve into the details of what suitable metrics might be, for this is a topic worthy of a thesis in and of itself. I do, however, maintain that the incorporation of the environmental aspect into our economic equation will involve a new and broader consideration of the way we think about our productive businesses, and our daily lives.

The preceding discussion regarding battery technology, alone, has shown the intricate and multifaceted connections between the supply of the necessary elements, competing industries, price, demand, and supply issues. If we are to successfully define economic metrics which are suitable and applicable, we need to consider the complete cycle of production, not just the presently employed linear input –output model . I suggest consideration of the biospheric model as an alternative, and that we attempt to move from an industrial linear economic analysis of environmental issues to a more complete model considering all inputs and outputs, such as in model depicted in Illustration 26 on the following page.

An inherent problem in using economic models to evaluate environmental policy is that we assume that we are dealing with the linearity of the economic model of production. And in doing so it is implicit that not only are efficiency and wealth our values upon which we make judgments, but also that only end products are of value. We concentrate on the consumer end products and not the actual end products which are the result of the production of consumer products - waste. In contrast, the cyclical biospheric model of production places value on all inputs and outputs of production, including waste.

As mentioned in the brief discussion on postmodernity, we need to review this in the historical context in which we find ourselves. I will not attempt to discuss or resolve the matter, for this is far beyond the scope of this discussion. But there are available, manageable concepts developed by contemporary scientists, economists and ecologists which succinctly address these issues. I re-

Illustration 26. The Biospheric and Linear Industrial Models of Production

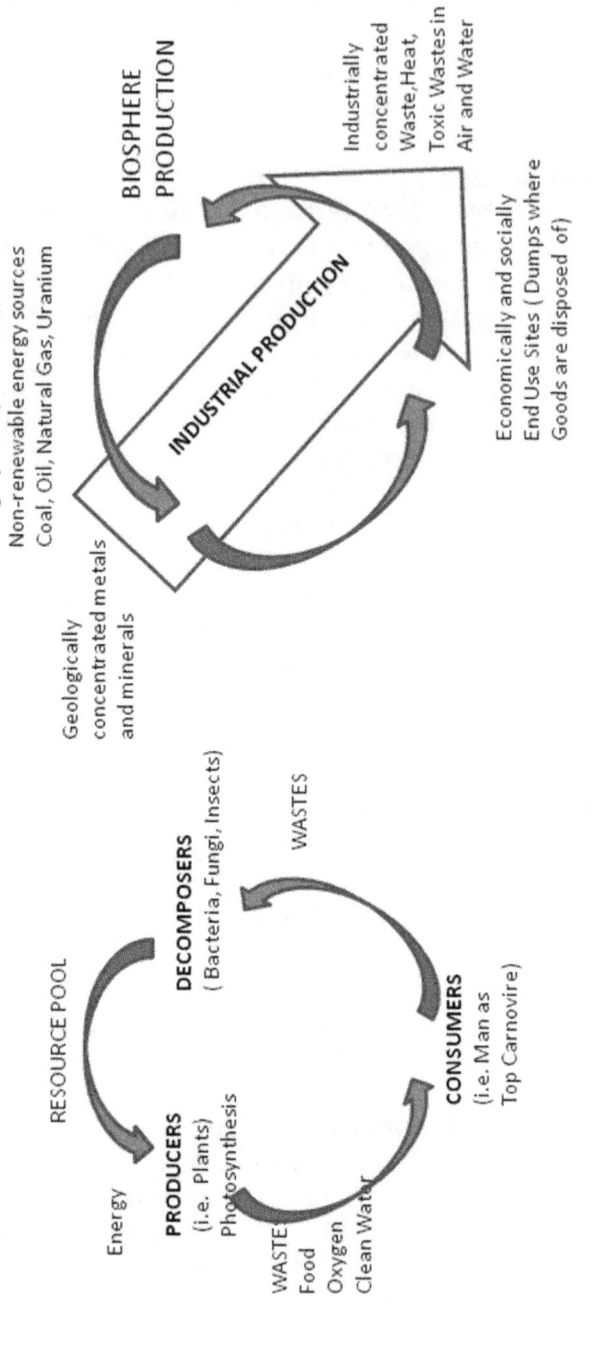

The BIOSPHERE Model of Production

The INDUSTRIAL Model of Production

Source: Gray 1994

fer to Amory Lovins and Wilfried Ver Eecke, as prime examples. Lovins, of Rocky Mountain Institute fame, has long maintained that, "simple changes in the way we run our businesses can yield startling benefits for today's shareholders and for future generations....The earth's ability to sustain life, and therefore economic activity, is threatened by the way we extract, process, transport, and dispose of a vast flow of resources....The economy, after all is embedded in the environment....Reducing the wasteful and destructive flow of resources from depletion to pollution represents a business opportunity." According to Lovins, we just have to get the numbers right (Lovins, Lovins and Hawkens 1999, 146).

Ver Eecke argues that the environment is a merit good, a good which is not a public good and which is requisite for human life, thereby allowing for governmental action to change market behavior in the instance of necessity.

> The market does not protect sufficiently against environmental harm because individual preferences (cheap but more polluting production method) that dramatically affect others (poisonous air, water or soil) are externalities that the market does not always capture, hence, their ill-effect is not captured in the price.
> One could argue that environmental protection is justifiable as a public good. It is a matter of internalizing bad externalities. There are, however, two arguments which show that the public good argument cannot cover all aspects of environmental protection measures. First, the method used to limit industrial pollution is not the method prescribed by public good's thinking. We do not ask consumers who want less pollution, how much they are willing to pay nor do we ask the polluters how much they would have to be paid to pollute less. Second, environment protection imposes an immediate cost. Hence, the government is in a position of having to correct the consumers' evaluation of the benefits of environmental protection. For these two reasons, environmental protection requires also merit good arguments that justify the government's right to interfere with consumer sovereignty (Ver Eecke 2010, 35-36).

If the environment is a merit good and if we demand, as evidenced by our behavior, accurate measures of costs and benefits, we may again be facing the dilemma of dealing with incommensurate ideas. This will require deliberation and discussion and, in the midterm, resolution through whatever consensus may be reached. The consensus cannot be the actuarial method of placing value on a single life lost to rising CO_2 emissions, but must take into account the value of economic measures which the government can enact, as suggested by Ver Eecke, to "interfere with consumer sovereignty (Ver Eecke 2011, 36). These measures include, but are not limited to, as per my proposals, an increase in taxes on gasoline at the federal level, deployment of available technology to make present passenger vehicles less pollutant, restriction of vehicles which do not meet CAFE standards, incentives for the development of non-polluting passenger vehicles, and the recreation of the American image of freedom in a new vision of active participation in a community dedicated to the preservation of the environment for our race.

This will require immense effort and cooperation and a change in our modus operandi at all levels, especially at the policy level, as suggested by Rycroft.

> ...Improving public technology policies will require better metaphors. In a world increasingly characterized by the coevolution of complex organizations and technologies, we need richer images that serve as conceptual scaffolding to underpin strategies and policies. Today we face a basic obstacle with how we conceptualize and are governed by categories. Our current categories have acquired a rigidity and permanence and most 'change' is merely an exercise in simplistic tinkering with existing building blocks. We live in an environment characterized by great ambiguity, with evolving and shifting forms and structures that are capable of embodying higher orders of collective insight and consensus. But in the area of complex technological innovation, these opportunities are often wasted as we try to understand and control factors and events that can't be understood (at least in detail) and can't be controlled with any degree of certainty. (Rycroft 2003, 9)

John Kitzhaber, former and newly re-elected Governor of the State of Oregon, described the problem: "Imagine, if you will, three overlapping circles—one representing economic needs, one representing environmental needs and one representing community social needs. The area where the three circles overlap is the area of sustainability, the area of livability—the area where all the threads of quality of life come together. If we are to 'have it all', we must recognize that these three circles are not separate, unrelated entities. Rather, they are the common desires and aspirations...and we must therefore strive to ensure that our efforts result in simultaneously meeting environmental, economic and community needs" (Kitzhaber 2011). (See Illustration 27, p. 130).

This discussion can be considered neither complete nor exhaustive, but it does highlight the myriad of issues involved in addressing environmental sustainability in the U.S. passenger car sector: vehicle technology, the availability of public transportation, corporate economics, consumer economics, consumer behavior, fuel prices, and the distribution of wealth, as well as the availability of rare resources.

Who determines the trade-offs - the winners and the losers, what is fair and equitable, what is even feasible, both technologically and economically - given the timeframe within concerted action must be taken?

If, as discussed in the section on Kant's moral philosophy, human life is absolutely valuable, then there can be no bargaining about its absolute worth. However, cost-benefit analyses treat people only "as locations at which wants may be found" and fail to treat them as value-havers and therefore are not a basis for legitimacy as such analyses and their results do not consider and are indifferent to true human values (Sagoff 1998, 333).

If we, as the only free agents on this planet, deny or are denied our absolute worth, there is no basis for morality. I have shown, through an investigation of Kant's moral philosophy, that we all have a binding moral duty to promote our own perfection and the happiness of others. If this holds for the individual by virtue of his human agency, then it must hold collectively for all human beings, present and future. Therefore, there exists a binding, intergenerational moral law and duty. This obligation is not contingent on the

Illustration 27. Kitzhaber's Three Spheres of Sustainability

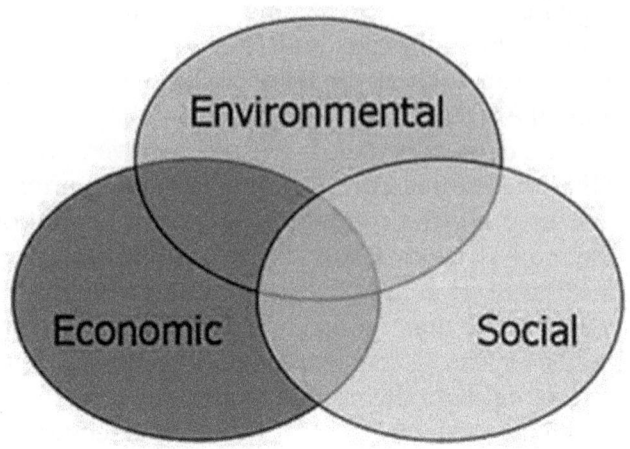

Source: Ithaca College 2010

time participation of people in history. This moral law requires that we must always act *unus pro omnibus, omnes pro uno* in the interest of all mankind, those human beings present today and those to come to maintain and guard those resources necessary for human life.

The challenges to the U.S. passenger car sector are daunting. Each of the sector participants has an integral role to play in meeting this challenge, especially the government which, I maintain, is called upon to take a stance and assume a role of central authority. The automobile producers are challenged to enter into new dialog of cooperation and communal effort to rapidly deploy existing technologies which are known to reduce CO_2 emissions. At the same time, they are called upon to the uttermost extent possible, to share thoughts, ideas, and concepts and to work together to expediently develop new vehicle technologies which do not contribute to CO_2 emissions and are not dependent on the valuable and scarce resources of the earth. The consumer is challenged to change his behavior and accept higher costs for the return of knowing we are doing all we can to help save the resources of our planet for each of us and for future generations.

We just might, in the words of Lovins, get the numbers right. We probably won't achieve this goal out of the box, but the alternative is to remain complacent and do nothing. Doing nothing also causes harm. I maintain, given the fact that we have the knowledge and tools to do so, that the promise lies in hope that we will, collectively, master this necessary and difficult challenge, not by "simplistic tinkering with existing building blocks" (Rycroft 2003, 9), but by mustering communal effort to use the great potential with which we are blessed in this country, to fulfill our duty to ourselves, our children, and the human race.

References

Adams, Richard. 1988. *The Eighth Day*. Austin University of Texas Press. Quoted in Arran Gare. *Postmodernism and the Environmental Crisis*, 5-6. New York: Routledge, 1996.

Amaden, Kimberly. 2011. Crude Oil Prices Definition. About.com. website. http://useconomy.about.com./od/economicindicators/p/Crude_Oil.htm. (accessed February 11, 2011).

Ambrosio, Francis. 2009. Class notes. *LSHV 603-01: The Challenge of Postmodernism*. Georgetown University (Fall Semester).

Amtrak. 2011. Amtrak website. http://tickets.amtrak.com/itd/amtrak. (accessed March 5, 2011).

Associated Press. 2010. Americans head OECD's obesity table. September 25. http://www.smh.com.au.world/americans-head-oecds-obesity-table-20100924- 15qmu.html. (accessed February 22, 2011).

———. 2011. U.S. Prices hit record high for time of year. *Washington Post*, February 12, A12.

Autoblog.com. 2011. Dual Clutch Basic Functional Diagram. Autobolg website. http://www.autoblog.com/2011/01/26/ford-details-power-shift-dual-clutch-tranny- for-2012-focus. (accessed March 1, 2011)

Automotive News. 2010. Key forms of electric vehicles, June 14, 34.

———. 2011. New Car Sales 2011, March 5. Automotive News website. http://search.autonews.com/search?q=2011+car+sales. (accessed March 5, 2011).

BBC News. 2010. Over 5 billion mobile phone connections worldwide. BBC News website. http://www.bbc.co.uk/news/10569081?print=true. (accessed February 28, 2011).

Blodget, Henry. 2005. Mine's Faster Than Yours – Riding Shanghai's maglev, the world's fastest train. *Slate*, March 21. Slate website. http://www.

slate.com/formatdynamics/CleanPrintProxy.aspx?1299261290934. (accessed March 4, 2011).

Bridbord , Kenneth and David Hanson. 2009. A Personal Perspective on the Initial Federal Health-Based Regulation to Remove Lead from Gasoline. *Environmental Health Perspectives*, Vol. 111, No. 8 (August): 1195 – 1201.

Carvel, John. 2002. Britons stand tall, if slightly heavy, in Europe. *Guardian*, August 28. Guardian website. http://www.guardian.co.uk/uk/2002/aug/28/science.research/print. (accessed February 24, 2011).

Center for Disease Control. 2009. Measured average height, weight, and waist circumference for adults ages 20 years and over. CDC website. http://www.cdc.gov/nchs/fastats/bodymeas.htm. (accessed February 24, 2011).

Chappell, Lindsay. 2011. Mahindra's poor mpg doesn't scare dealers. *Automotive News*, February 21, 6.

Crain, Keith. 2010. Electric cars won't spark big sales. *Automotive News*, March 29, 12.

———. 2011. Electric cars will have a role. *Automotive News*, February 21, 12

Davies, Richard. 1975. *The Age of Asphalt: The Automobile, the Freeway, and the Condition of Metropolitan America*. Edited by Harold Hyman. Philadelphia: J.P. Lippencott Company.

Dawson, Chester and Mike Ramsey. 2010. Toyota, Honda unveil new electric cars. *Wall Street Journal*, November 18. Wall Street Journal website. http://online.wjs.com/article/SB10001424052748704648604575621430120181738.html. (accessed February 17, 2011).

Dessler, Andrew, and Edward Parson. 2007. *The Science and Politics of Global Climate Change*. New York: Cambridge University Press.

Durlauf, Steven. 1998. What Should Policy Makers Know About Economic Complexity? *The Washington Quarterly*, Vol. 21, No. 1 (Winter): 157 - 165.

Early Electric Car Site. 2010. Electric Car Companies of the World (by Brand) before 1940. Early Electric Car website. http://www.earltelectric.com/carcompanies.html. (accessed February 24, 2010).

Economist. 2009. The biggest obstacle to a climate-change bill is rural America. *The Economist*, November 14, 44.

———. 2010a. Hub of the Matter. *The Economist*, April 24, 78 - 79.

———. 2010b. Highly charged motoring. *The Economist*, October 9, 23.

———. 2010c. High-speed trains – Running out of speed. *The Economist*, December 11, 40.

Eilperin, Juliet. 2010. First half of 2010 sets record heat. *Washington Post*, July 20, E3.

Ford, Henry II. 1956. We Can Do Something About Highways, Traffic, and Safety: Notes for a Talk. Quoted in Cotten Seiler. *Republic of Drivers – A Cultural History of Automobility in America*, 101. Chicago: University of Chicago Press, 2008.

Ford Motor Company.1956. *Freedom of the American Road*. Quoted in Cotten Seiler. *Republic of Drivers – A Cultural History of Automobility in America*, 99. Chicago University of Chicago Press, 2008.

_____. 2011. Ford Motor Company website. http://www.ford.com/vehicles/. (accessed March 1, 2011).

GangHe, Gang. 2008. Finding a Safe Level of Carbon Dioxide for the Global Atmosphere: Results of the Tällberg Forum. World Resource Institute: *Earth Trends* (September). World Research Institute website. http://earthtrends.wri.org/updates/node/320. (accessed December 2010).

Gare, Arran. 1996. *Postmodernism and the Environmental Crisis*. New York: Routledge, 1995. Reprint, New York: Routledge (page references are to the reprint edition).

Global Lead Network. 2011. Global Lead Network: The Secret History of Lead: Ethyl- Octel Family Tree. Global Lead Network website. http://globalleadnet.com/136/the-secret-istory-of-lead-ethyl-octel-family-tree. (accessed February 6, 2011).

Gordon, Deborah and Daniel Sperling. 2010. Big Oil can't get beyond petroleum. *Washington Post*, June 13, B1, B3.

Gray, Elizabeth. 1994. Come Inside The Circle of Creation: The Ethic of Attunement. In *Ethics and Environmental Policy: Theory Meets Practice* ed. Frederick Ferré and Peter Hartel , 21-41. Athens: The University of Georgia Press, 2003.

Greene, Joshua. 2003. From Neural 'is' to 'ought': What Are the Moral Implications of Neuroscientific Moral Psychology? *Nature Reviews Neuroscience*, Vol. 4 (October): 847 - 852.

Guilford, Dave. 2010a. Consumer is the wild card in mpg game. *Automotive News*, March 22, 24.

_____. 2010b. For new CAFE, automakers place high-stake tech bets. *Automotive News*, March 22, 1, 25.

_____. 2010c. Some feel 'footprint' plan should get the boot. *Automotive News*, March 22, 24.

_____. 2011. $5-a-gallon gas? Execs strategize. *Automotive News*, January 17, 22.

Hampton, Keith. 2009. Quoted in Bill McKibben. *Eaarth: Making a Life on a Tough New Planet*, 203. New York: Times Books Henry Holt and Company, LLC, 2010.

Heining, Duncan. 1998. Cars and Girls – The Car, Masculinity, and Pop

Music. In *The Motor Car and Popular Culture in the 20th Century*. David Thoms, Len Holden, and Tim Claydon, 96 - 119. Brookfield: Ashgate Publishing Company, 1998.

Heinzerling, Amy. 2010. Global Carbon Dioxide Emissions Fall in 2009 – Past Decade Still Sees Rapid Emissions Growth. Earth Policy Institute website. http://earth-policy.org/index.php?/indicators/C52/#. (accessed January 18, 2011).

Hoffman, Paul.1939. America Goes to Town. *Saturday Evening Post*, April 29, 4. Quoted in David St. Clair. *The Motorization of American Cities*, 122. New York:Praeger Publishers, 1986.

Holden, Len.1998. More Than a Marque. The Car as Symbol: Aspects of Culture and Ideology. In *The Motor Car and Popular Culture in the 20th Century*. David Thoms, Len Holden, and Tim Claydon, 28 – 40. Brookfield: Ashgate Publishing Company, 1998.

Homer-Dixon, Thomas.1999. *Environment, Scarcity, and Violence*. New Jersey: Princeton University Press.

Hybridcars. 2008. The Hybrid Car Battery: A Definitive Guide. Hybridcars website. http://www.hybridcars.com/hybrid-car-battery. (accessed March 1, 2011).

_____. 2009. 2011 CAFE Targets Drop Below Level of Today's Cars. Hybridcars website, March 27. http://hybridcars.com/incentives-laws/cafe-targets-2011-drop- 25684.html. (accessed February 16, 2011).

Hybrid Vehicle Organization. 2010. Hybrid Vehicle History More Than a Century of Evolution and Refinement. Hybrid Vehicle Organization website. http://www.hybrid-vehicle-org./hybrid-vehicle-history.html. (accessed February 24, 2010).

Innospec Inc. 2011. Innospec FAQs. Innospec website. http://www.innospecinc.com/corporate-overview/faqs.html. (accessed February 25, 2011).

Ithaca College. 2010. Presentation of Diagram of Kitzhaber's Three Circles of Sustainability. Ithica website. http://www.ithica,edu/sustainability. (accessed May 1, 2010).

JATO Dynamics. 2010. US Car Market Still Almost Twice As Polluting As Europe and Japan. Press release. green autoblog website. http://green.autoblog.com/2010/06/16/u-s-is-sadly-number-one-when-it-comes-to- co2-emissions/html. (accessed January 25, 2011).

Jerram, Lisa. 2010. More on Rare Earth Metals: Are They the New Oil? *Hybridcars*, December 20. Hybridcars website. http://www.hybridcars.com/news/more-rare-earth-metals-are-they-the-new-oil-29074.html. (accessed March 6, 2011).

Jones, David. 2008. *Mass Motorization + Mass Transit An American History and Policy Analysis*. Bloomington: Indiana University Press.

Kant, Immanuel. 1993a. *Critique of Practical Reason*, 3d ed. Translated by Lewis White Beck. Upper Saddle River: Prentice Hall.

———. 1993b. *Grounding for the Metaphysics of Morals*, 3d ed. Translated by James W. Ellington. Indianapolis: Hackett Publishing Co.

———. 1993c. *Lecture on Ethics*.Translated by James W. Ellington. Indianapolis:Hackett Publishing Co.

———. 1996. *The Metaphysics of Morals*. Cambridge: Cambridge University Press.

———. 2005. *Religion and Rational Theology*. Translated by Allen Wood and George Di Giovanni. Cambridge: Cambridge University Press. First published 1996.

———. 2007. *Critique of Pure Reason*. Translated by Norman Smith. New York: Palgrave Macmillan.Original edition, Palgrave Macmillan, 1929.

Kennedy, John. 1960. Campaign address, Valley Forge PA, October 29. John F. Kennedy Presidential Library and Museum website. http://www.jfklibrary.org/Research/Ready-Reference/JFK-Quotations.aspx. (accessed February 28, 2011).

Kitman, Jamie. 2000. 8,500 Years of Lead…79 Years of Leaded Gasoline. *The Nation*, March 20. The Nation website. http://www.thenation.com/doc/20000320/timeline. (accessed February 24, 2010).

Kitzhaber, John. 2001. Sustainable Forests Speech at Oregon State University, October 18. http://www.oregon.gov/ODF/BOARD/kitzhaber.shtml. (accessed May 1,2010).

Klein, David. 2001. Positive Feedback, Lock-in, and Environmental Policy. *PolicySciences* Vol. 34, 95 – 107.

Kranz, Rick. 2010a. Industry expects fuel cells on U.S. highways in 2015. *Automotive News*, June 14, 20H.

———. 2010b. Today's gas-burners must cut energy loss. *Automotive News*, June 14, 20J.

Lasse, Todd. 2010. Comparing America's Top 10 Best-Selling Vehicles, 2009 vs. 2000. *Motor Trend*, October. Motor Trend website.. http://www.motortrend.com/features/auto_news/2010/112_1004?america_top_10_best_selling_vehicle_comparison_2009_2000. (accessed February 24, 2011).

Leed, Eric. 1991. *The Mind of the Traveler: From Gilgamesh to Global Tourism*. New York: Basic Books.

Lewis, Latif. 2010. Gas Prices Around the World: What It Costs to Fill 'Er Up. *Daily Finance*. Daily Finance website. http://www.dailyfinance.com/story/gas-prices- around-the-world/19543148/. (accessed January 24, 2011).

Lovins, Amory, L. Hunter Lovins, and Paul Hawken. 1999. A Road Map

References

for Natural Capitalism. *Harvard Busines Review*, May-June, 145-158.

Lyotard, Jean-François. 1984. *The Postmodern Condition: A Report on Knowledge.* Ed. Wlad Godzich and Jochen Schulte-Sasse. Vol. 10, *Theory and History of Literature.* Translated by Geoff Bennington and Brian Massumi. Minneapolis: University of Minnesota Press

Manning, T. 1995. Driving along in my automobile. *New Statesman and Society*, April 14, 33-35. Quoted in David Thoms, Len Holden, Tim Claydon. *The Motor Car and Popular Culture in the 20th Century*, 30. Brookfield: Ashgate Publishing Company, 1998.

Marsh, Peter and Peter Collett. 1986. *Driving Passion: The Psychology of the Car.* London: Jonathan Cape. Quoted in David Thoms, Len Holden, Tim Claydon. *The Motor Car and Popular Culture in the 20th Century*, 30. Brookfield: Ashgate Publishing Company, 1998.

McKibben, Bill. 2010. *Eaarth: Making a Life on a Tough New Planet.* New York: Times Books Henry Holt and Company, LLC.

Merriam Webster Online Dictionary. http://www.merriam-webster.com/dictionary/ought. (accessed January 17, 2010).

Miller, John and Scott Page. 2007. *Complex Adaptive Systems: An Introduction to Computational Models of Social Life.* New Jersey: Princeton University Press.

Miller, Josh. 2011. Toyota Hybrid to get lithium ion batteries. *Automotive News*, January 31. http://reviews.cnet.com/8301-13746_7-20030072-48.html. (accessed March 1, 2011).

Mufson, Steven. 2011a. Coal's burnout. *Washington Post*, January 2, G1, G5.

_____. 2011b. Debt across U.S. hits post-WWII levels. *Washington Post*, February 23, A10.

Mui, Simon, Jeff Alson, Benjamin Ellies, and David Ganss. 2007. A Wedge Analysis of the U.S. Transportation Sector. U.S. Environmental Protection Agency EPA420- R-07-007.

National Highway Traffic Safety Administration. 2011. CAFE Overview – Frequently Asked Questions. NHTSA website. http://www.nhtsa.gov/cars/rules/cafe/overview.htm. (accessed February 14, 2011).

National Oceanic and Atmospheric Administration. 2011. Atmospheric CO2 Mauna Loa Observatory (Scripps/NOAA/ESRL) Monthly & Annual Mean CO2 Concentrations (ppm) March 1958 – present. CO2 Now Website. http://co2now.org/Current-CO2/CO2-Now/Current-Data-for-Atomspheric- CO2.html. (accessed January 7, 2011).

Newport, Frank. 2009. Americans: Economy Takes Precedence Over Environment. Gallup website. http://gallup.com/poll/116962/Americans-Economy-Takes-Precedence-Environment,aspx. (accessed December 12, 2009).

Nissan. 2011. XTRONIC CVT. Nissan website. http://www.nissanglobal.

com/EN/TECHNOLOGY/OVERVIEW/cvt.html. (accessed March 1, 2011).

Orbitz. 2011. Orbitz website. http://www.orbitz.com/App/ViewFlightSe archResults?retrieveParams=true&z=dbe5&r=6k&z=dbe7&r=6m&last Page=interstitial.(accessed March 5, 2011).

Organization of the Petroleum Exporting Countries. 2011. Member Countries. OPEC website, http://www.opec.org/opec_web/en/about_us/25.htm. (accessed February 23, 2011).

Pennsylvania Project High Speed Maglev. 2011. Pennsylvania Project High Speed Maglev website. http://www.maglevpa.com/plan/html. (accessed March 2, 2011).

Pew Center on Global Climate Change. 2010. Increasing the Energy Efficiency of Vehicles - Taking Climate Change into Account in U.S. Transportation – Increasing the Energy Efficiency of Vehicles. Pew website. http://www.pewclimate.org/print/policy_center/policy_reports_and_analysis/brief_us_transportation/vehicles.cfm. (accessed December 18, 2010).

Report of the American Physical Society Panel on Public Affairs and the Materials Research Society. 2011. *Energy Critical Elements: Securing Materials for Emerging Technologies.* By Robert Jaffe, chairman, et al. APS website. http://www.aps.org/policy/reports/popa- reports/loader.cfm?csModule=security/getfile&PageID=236337. (accessed February 20, 2011).

Research and Innovative Technology Administration, Bureau of Transportation Statistics. 2010. Average Fuel Efficiency of U.S. Passenger Cars and Light Trucks. RITA website. http://www.bts.gov/cgi-bin/breadcrumbs/PrintVersion_redesign.cgi. (accessed February 21, 2011).

Reuscher, John. 2010. Class notes. *LSHV 392-01: The Ethics of Aristotle and Kant.* Georgetown University (Spring Semester).

Reynolds, Terrence. 2009. Class notes. *LSHV 602-01: The Rise of the Modern Spirit.* Georgetown University (Spring Semester).

Roland, Neil. 2011. Obama puts EVs over hydrogen fuel-cell cars. *Automotive News*, February 21, 8.

Romney, George. 1950. The Motor Vehicle and the Highway: Some Historical Implications. In Highways in our National Life: A Symposium., ed. Jean Labatut and Wheaton Lace, 221. Princeton: Princeton University Press. Quoted in Cotton Seiler. *Republic of Drivers – A Cultural History of Automobility in America*, 95. Chicago: University of Chicago Press.

Rosenberg, Mica and Eduardo Garcia. 2011. Known lithium deposits can cover electric car boom. *Reuters,* February 11. Reuters website. http://reuters.com/assets/print?aid=USTRE61A5AY20100211. (accessed February 23, 2001).

Rutledge, Ian. 2006. *Addicted to Oil*. London: L. B. Tauris & Co.
Rycroft, Robert. 2003. *Innovation Networks and Complex Technologies: Policy Implications of the Unknown, and the Unknowable*. The George Washington University Center for the Study of Globalization.
Sagoff, Mark. 1998. At the Shrine of our Lady of Fatima, or Why Political Questions Are Not All Economic. In *The Environmental Ethics and Policy Book*, ed. Donald VanDeVeer and Christine Pierce, 327 - 335. Belmont: Wadsworth/Thompson Learning.
St. Clair, David. 1986. *The Motorization of American Cities*. New York: Praeger Publishers.
Sampson, Pamela. 2011. World stocks advance on earnings, higher oil price. *Business Week*, February 1. Business Week website. http://www.businessweek.com/ap/financialnews/D9L3SO401.htm. (accessed February 1, 2011).
SBI Energy. 2010. High Speed Rail Infrastructure Component Manufacturing, July. SBI website. http://www.sbireports.com/High-Speed-Rail-2496796/. (accessed March 4, 2011).
Schaeffler Group. 2008. World Premiere: LuK dual dry clutch 7-speed DSG gearbox in volume production at Volkswagen. Press release, February 13. Schaeffler Group website. HTTP://WWW.LUK.DE/CONTENT.LUK.DE/EN/PRESS/PRESS-RELEASES/PRESS-DETAILS.JSP?ID=2405783. (accessed March 1, 2011).
_____. 2010. UniAir/MultiAir, the world's first fully-variable hydraulic valve control system. Press release, January 11. Schaeffler Group website. http://www.schaeffler.com/content.schaefflergroup.de/en/press/pressreleases/standardsuche/pressreleasedetail.jsp?id=3359243. (accessed March 1, 2011).
Scharchburg, Richard.2011. *Charles F. Kettering : Doing the right thing at the right time*. Kettering University website. http://www.kettering.edu/visitors/about/charles_kettering.jsp. (accessed January 25, 2011).
Seiler, Cotten. 2008. *Republic of Drivers – A Cultural History of Automobility in America*. Chicago: University of Chicago Press.
Shanghai Maglev Transportation Development Co., Ltd. 2011. Shanghai Maglev Transportation Development Co., Ltd. website. http://www.smtdc.com/en/xnlv2.asp. (accessed March 4, 2011).
Shore, Sandy and Chris Kahn. 2011. Gas prices climbing despite hefty supply. *USA Today*, February 11. USA Today website. http://www.usatoday.com/cleanprint/?1297553636514. (accessed February 12, 2011).
Sim, Stuart, ed. 2009. *The Routledge Companion to Postmodernism*. 2d ed. New York: Routledge, 2005. Reprint, New York: Routledge (page references are to the reprint edition).
Simpkins, Jason. 2011. Oil Companies Pumping Profits as Crude Contin-

ues to Climb. *Money Morning*, January 28. Money Morning website. http://www.marketoracle.co.uk/Article25917.html. (accessed February 2, 2011).

Slater, Cliff. 1997. General Motors and the Demise of the Streetcars. *Transportation Quarterly*, Vol. 51, No. 3 (Summer): 45 – 66.

Society of Automotive Engineers International. History of Fuel Cells. SAE International website. http://www.sae.org/fuelcells/fuelcells-history.htm. (accessed February 24, 2010).

⎯⎯⎯⎯. 2011. GM, LG Chem license Argonne chemistry or next-gen lithium batteries. *Automotive Engineering International*, February 1, 9-10.

Socolow, Robert and Stephen Pacala. 2004. Stabilization Wedges: Solving the Climate Problem for the Next 50 Years with Current Technologies. *Science*, Vol. 305 (August): 968 - 972.

⎯⎯⎯⎯. 2006.A Plan to Keep Carbon in Check. *Scientific American* (September): 50 - 63.

Stein, Jason and Bradford Wernie. 2011. Getting to 35.5: The ABCs of mpg. *Automotive News*, January 3, 1, 24.

Thoms, David, Len Holden, and Tim Claydon. 1998. *The Motor Car and Popular Culture in the 20th Century*. Brookfield: Ashgate Publishing Company.

Tidwell, Mike. 2011. Weather beaten. *Washington Post*, February 27, B1, B5.

Time Magazine. 1957. National Affairs: The Du Pont Case. *Time Magazine*, June 17. Time website. http://www.time.com.time/time/printout/0,8816,867705,00.html. (accessed February 7, 2011).

United States Department of Energy. 2010. Criticals Material Strategy. December 9. DOE website. http://www.energy.gov/news/documents/criticalmaterialsstrategy.pdf. (accessed February 2, 2011).

⎯⎯⎯⎯. 2011. Energy Efficiency & Renewable Energy, Transmission Technologies. DOE website. http://www.fueleconomy.gov/feg/tech_transmission.shtml. (accessed March 4, 2011).

United States Department of the Interior, Bureau of Land Management. 2011. Qs and As About Oil and Gas Leasing. BLM website.http://www.blm.gov/wo/st/en/prog/energy/oil_and_gas/questions_and_answers.prnt.html(accessed February 28, 2011).

United States Department of the Interior, Bureau of Ocean Energy Management. 2011. BOEMRE website. http://www.boemre.gov/topics/topic-index.htm. (accessed February 28, 2011).

United States Department of Transportation. 2009.1990 Nationwide Personal Transportation Survey: Summary of Travel Trends. FHWA-PL-92-027. Table8.6.

United States Department of Transportation, Federal Railroad Administration. 2011.Vision of High-Speed Rail in America. Press Release April 16. FRA website. http://www.fra.dot.gov/rpd/passenger/31.shtml.(accessed February 27, 2011).

United States Energy Information Administration. Office of Oil and Gas, U.S. Department of Energy. 1997. Petroleum 1996 Issues and Trends. DOE/EIA-0615. EIA website. http://tonto.eia.doe.gov/ftproot/petroleum/061596.pdf. (accessed February 5, 2011).

―――――. 2011a. Oil Market Basics – Supply. EIA website. http://www.eia.doe.gov/pub/oil_gas/petroleum/analysis_publications/oil_market_basics/supply_text.htm. (accessed February 12, 2011).

―――――. 2011b. Crude Oil and Total Petroleum Imports Top 15 Countries. EIA website. http://www.eia.doe.gov/pbu/oil_gas/petroleum/data_publications/company_level_imports. (accessed February 16, 2011).

―――――. 2011c. Short Term Energy Outlook. EIA website. http://www.eia.doe/gov/petroleum/index/cfm. (accessed February 28, 2011).

―――――. 2011d. Federal and State Motor Fuel Taxes. Table EN1. *Petroleum Marketing Monthly*, March, 153

United States Environmental Protection Agency. 1996. EPS Takes Final Step in Phaseout of Leaded Gasoline. Press Release. EPA website. http://www.epa.gov/history/topics/lead/o2.htm. (accessed February 7, 2011).

―――――. 2005. Greenhouse Gas Emissions from a Typical Passenger Vehicle. EPA 420-F-05-001. EPA website. http://www.epa.gov/oms/climate/420f05004.pdf.html. (accessed January 24, 2011).

―――――. 2010a. Inventory of U.S. Gas Emissions and Sinks: 1990 – 2008. EPA 430- R- 10-006. EPA website. http://www.epa.gov/climatechange/emissions/usgginventory.html. (accessed   January 24, 2011).

―――――. 2010b. EPA and NHTSA to Propose Greenhouse Gas and Fuel Efficiency   Standards for Heavy-Duty Trucks; Begin Process for Further Light-Duty Standards. EPA -420-F-10-038, May 2010.

Van De Veer, Donald and Christine Pierce, eds. 2003. *The Environmental Ethics & Policy Book*. 3d ed. Toronto: Nelson Thomson Learning.

Vastag, Brian. 2011. U.S. action urged to safeguard supply of rare materials. *Washington Post*, February 20, A6.

Ver Eecke, Wilfried. 2010. Merit Goods and Business Ethics, Draft February.

Volkswagen. Volkswagen website. http://www.vw.com/en/models.html. (accessed   March 1, 2011).

Walkley, David and Theodore Zimmerman. 1958. Clayton Section 7 and the DuPont- GM Case: A "Big Stick" for Antitrust? California Law Review, Vol. 46, Mo. 2 (May): 266 – 276.

Wall Street Journal. 2011. What's Moving U.S. Auto Sales. *Wall Street Jour-*

nal Online, March 1. http://online.wsj.com/mdc/public/page/2_3022-autosales.html.

Whoriskey, Peter. 2010. Industry's rebound more SUV than mpg. *Washington Post,* December 30, A1, A16.

———. 2011a. Bailed-out GM, Chrysler push back on fuel economy. *Washington Post,* January 14, A17.

———. 2011c. A pricey plan to boost sales of electric cars. *Washington Post,* January 27, A12.

Womack, James, Daniel Jones, Daniel Roos, and Donna Carpenter. 1990. *The Machine That Changed The World.* New York: Rawson Associates.

World Bank. 2010. World Development Indicators, updated December 21, 2010. World Bank website. http://data.worldbank.ord/indicatore/ENATM.CO2E.PC?cid=GDP_27.html. (accessed January 25, 2011).

World Health Organization. 2010. Estimated BMI for Males over 15, 2010. WHO website. http://apps.who.int/bmi/index.jsp. (AccessedFebruary 22, 2011).

———. 2011. Health Topics – Obesity. WHO website.http://www.who.int/topics/obesity/en. (accesed February 22, 2011).

Wright, Richard. 1970. Responsibility for the Ecological Crisis. *Bioscience,* 1 (August): 851 - 853.

Yacobucci, Brent and Robert Bamberger. 2007. Automobile and Light Truck Fuel Economy: The CAFE Standards. Congressional Research Service.

www.ingramcontent.com/pod-product-compliance
Lightning Source LLC
Chambersburg PA
CBHW031315150426
43191CB00005B/244